Sustaining Identity, Recapturing Heritage

Sustaining Identity, Recapturing Heritage

Exploring Issues of Public History, Tourism, and Race in a Southern Town

Ann Denkler

LEXINGTON BOOKS

A division of
ROWMAN & LITTLEFIELD PUBLISHERS, INC.
Lanham • Boulder • New York • Toronto • Plymouth, UK

LEXINGTON BOOKS

A division of Rowman & Littlefield Publishers, Inc.
A wholly owned subsidary of The Rowman & Littlefield Publishing Group, Inc.
4501 Forbes Boulevard, Suite 200
Lanham, MD 20706

Estover Road
Plymouth PL6 7PY
United Kingdom

British Library Cataloguing in Publication Information Available

Library of Congress Cataloging-in-Publication Data

Denkler, Ann, 1965–
   Sustaining identity, recapturing heritage : exploring issues of public history, tourism,
and race in a southern town / Ann Denkler.
      p. cm.
   Includes bibliographical references and index.
   ISBN-13: 978-0-7391-1991-4 (cloth : alk. paper)
   ISBN-10: 0-7391-1991-5 (cloth : alk. paper)
   1. Luray (Va.)—History. 2. Luray (Va.)—Historiography. 3. Public history—
Virginia—Luray. 4. Historic sites—Interpretive programs—Virginia—Luray. I. Title.
   F234.L87D46 2007
   305.8009755'94—dc22   2007028823

Printed in the United States of America

⊗™ The paper used in this publication meets the minimum requirements of American
National Standard for Information Sciences—Permanence of Paper for Printed Library
Materials, ANSI/NISO Z39.48-1992.

Contents

Introduction

Public history sites—markers, monuments, memorials, historic houses, national parks, battlefields, and museums—are a vital and revealing part of the American landscape. Far more than simply symbols of the past, public history sites reflect our hopes, disappointments, dreams, and expectations as individuals and as a nation. They encompass personal and collective memory and bind communities and our nation together. Over the course of a century, Americans have traveled thousands of miles and spent millions of dollars to see these visible vestiges of our past and experience a diverse range of histories and heritage.

Within the last quarter century, however, public history sites have come under intense scrutiny. Fueled by the Civil Rights and women's rights movements, poststructural thought, and the disintegration of white male literary and historical canons, anthropologists, tourism scholars, writers, artists, environmentalists, and historians have decried some public history sites as exclusive, vacuous spaces that very often exhibit false history, and labeled the tourists who visit these sites passive and willing participants. Consider historian James W. Loewen's recent work, *Lies Across America: What Our Historic Sites Get Wrong,* which unravels myths behind many sites with a humorous slant, and David Lowenthal's *Possessed by the Past: The Heritage Crusade and the Spoils of History*, which offers a vituperative view of the evils heritage can produce.[1] For Lowenthal, where history "aims to reduce bias, heritage strengthens it."[2] Heritage, he argues, is based mostly on collective beliefs stemming from a nineteenth-century nationalism which "roused mass allegiance to icons of collective identity."[3] Poststructural archaeologists and critics Michael Shanks and Christopher Tilley argue that historic sites tell nothing about the past; they are made meaningful in the present for political reasons, usually by members of the elite.[4]

1

Individuals in Luray, Virginia and all over the country continue to create and consume heritage. Residents of historic houses, for example, apply and pay for the privilege of hanging a historic plaque on an outside wall indicating their place in the history of the house and the community. Millions of visitors travel to Colonial Williamsburg and accept, at high prices, selective versions of history. In Luray, a small rural town (population 4,800) situated in the northern section of the Shenandoah Valley in northwestern Virginia and the focus of my study, heritage is reflected in historic houses, monuments to Confederate soldiers, and even in an unimposing square stone—a purported slave auction block.

In this book, I argue that heritage and public history, especially relating to the German-Swiss founding families and Confederate soldiers in Luray, are vital components to white individual and white community identity and are reflected in its commemorative landscape, or spaces where humans have manipulated the natural world for the purposes of commemorating an historic event or historical actors.[5] In contrast to some communities that have lost aspects of their cultural identity and landscape to meet the demands of outside groups—missionaries, government officials, and tourists—Luray, which has also seen its share of these groups, has been able to resist large-scale change and impose its own conceptions of heritage on the landscape and on historical and tourism literature (figure 1).

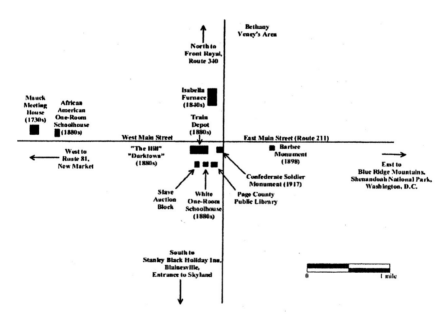

Map of prominent public history sites in downtown Luray, Virginia.
(Illustration by Bernard K. Means)

Figure 1.   Luray History Map

In establishing a definition of the term commemorative landscapes, I use the philosophy that landscapes are seen, and, more importantly, are conceptualized differently from person to person to explore the multiplicity of meanings and symbolism of commemorative landscapes in Luray.[6] I also relied upon ideas developed by academics, who assert that historical studies should be pursued with an "ethnographic" or performance approach.[7] By looking at people of the past as "actors" and their landscapes as "stage settings," this type of methodology can uncover the rich potential for studying the *dynamic* relationship between actors and their material worlds, including their commemorative landscapes.

I also argue that the tourist brochures, narratives, homes, and monuments—all aspects of public history—devoted to the founding families and Confederate soldiers dominate heritage in Luray and marginalize the history and heritage of African Americans and American Indians. The public history, then, does not reflect the true history of this town or who contributed to its foundation. This conclusion, as James Loewen and other cultural critics have found, is not necessarily new, especially pertaining to the glorification of the Lost Cause above all else in the South. Academics and popular literature have wrestled with this phenomenon since the Civil War ended and continue to do so today. What I add to this burgeoning crop of work, however, is a more nuanced view of what historians, cultural critics, and others call, simply, the "South" by focusing on one town and looking at the interplay of history, public history, race, and tourism. A close look at one town helps bring out the fact that the South should not and cannot be defined in monolithic terms, and neither should its devotion to the Lost Cause. The region of this study, Luray, Virginia in the Shenandoah Valley, is a distinctive geographic and socioeconomic region in the South, and possesses its own discrete "southernness"; it has even been labeled the "Third South."[8] Since much of the Valley was settled in the eighteenth century by Pennsylvania migrants, and it established strong trade networks in and with the North, its ties to the South and its "southernness" are tenuous and questionable. Also, the Valley's relationship to slavery is unique since the absence of a single crop agricultural system and dominance of yeoman farmers as opposed to plantation masters has led historians to claim that slavery—and the African American presence here—is meaningless.

Like many southern communities, no African American structures or sites are designated as historic or are included in the town's tourist literature, even though Luray contains nineteenth-century African American churches and schools, among other structures. In fact, in most areas of the Shenandoah Valley, the absence of African American history and culture is prevalent. Some of my white informants thought that African American history was ignored in Luray because slavery—a discourse used by my research sources to frame the African American experience here—was not a major historical event in the Valley. The reason, according to some local historians of the past and present, is that the expansive plantations in Tidewater, Virginia, with large numbers of enslaved people, and the large African American population in Richmond, the state capitol, have overshadowed the presence of African Americans in the Valley. Importantly, the wheat culture that helped to create the Valley, also contributed to the settlement of African Americans as slaves and free blacks. This type of agricultural system yielded a distinct form of slavery and a free black labor, as I will demonstrate, further defining the Valley as a distinct cultural region. None of this historical data is public history—yet. I suggest that incorporating a more equitable representation of history to display in public means telling these stories—of wheat production, of iron production, and slavery and telling stories that reveal just how common our white and African American histories are.

As I began to research public history sites I discovered hidden or untold stories of slaves or habitation by African Americans. I noticed, for example, that free blacks and enslaved African Americans worked alongside whites in an iron furnace, and that African American workers at the furnace were most likely the original settlers of West Main Street, considered the "Black" section of town. But this shared history does not translate into a shared heritage: the commemorative landscape excludes mention of African Americans, leaving much of their history hidden. I suggest, however, that in this surreptitious state, marginalized celebrations can serve as empowering, and should and could be considered a new angle of "public history."

Recent tourism literature offers a cutting-edge, postmodern perspective on the politics of tourism and cultural identity, rejecting the idea of tourism impact in favor of a system of the various actors in a touristic situation—locals, scholars, and outsiders—involved in networks of collusion and cooperation over time. This view shows that locals and tourists have a long history of more cooperative, less exploitative types of relationships.[9] In Luray, I argue that local citizens have historically been able to resist change from generations of tourists, and cultural commodification. That is, they have been able to determine how they want their town and culture to be lived for themselves and on public view.

Dona Brown provocatively explores regional tourism in *Inventing New England: Regional Tourism in the Nineteenth Century*. Her discovery—that tourism in nineteenth-century Nantucket created an identity of "quaintness" for the natives—supports the existence of a dialectical relationship between tourism and cultural identity. She believes that ". . . local history and culture were a crucial part of the tourist industry," but were, ". . . ultimately at the service of the industry."[10] Brown aptly demonstrates how power and class relationships framed tourism in Nantucket.

Brown is left wondering if the indigenous Nantucketers knew about the recreation of their identities. She writes, "And those on the front lines of the transformation, the people who were most often mentioned by guidebooks as "quaint," have left no traces of their own thoughts."[11] Because my study centers on ethnography, I was able to ask "those on the front line" about the effects of tourism on their history and identities. My ethnographic work with this population revealed that it is not the tourists who visit Luray and stay for a day or a week, or just lunch who are not welcome; it is the recent influx of retirees from Northern Virginia and the eastern corridor who visit and decide to stay. These "postmodern" tourists, or new citizens who are treated as perpetual visitors, are the most threatening and disliked type of tourist because of their desire to change things in Luray.[12] They encourage the construction of stores, or demand that the smell of chicken litter emanating from nearby poultry farms be eliminated. Tourists who come to Luray and the Shenandoah National Park are not as dangerous to the local culture as the postmodern tourists who threaten to transform the agricultural character of the town. This type of tourism is important to study since more and more small, rural communities in selected regions of the United States are battling with sprawl and waves of city dwellers wishing to relocate to these areas.

Part of what also lies hidden in the history books and commemorative landscapes are the stories and experiences of African Americans as tourists, and as active members of the tourism trade in Luray and the Shenandoah National Park throughout the twentieth century. If tourist scholarship is now expanding to include a much more nuanced and diachronic perspective, it still lacks discussion of African Americans as travelers and tourists. This absence was something I had never considered until I began ethnographic and primary research in Luray and discovered the presence of tourist cabins for African Americans and even a designated "colored" mountain for African Americans in the segregated Shenandoah National Park (SNP). Thus, the African American tourism experience, at its core, was separate and not equal.

This book drew on myriad primary sources, especially the *Page News and Courier (PN&C),* first printed in the late 1800s. On microfilm at the public library (and unfortunately not catalogued), this weekly newspaper was a goldmine of information, as it not only covers local history over a one-hundred year period, but helped me to verify oral history accounts of various events, including the dedication and rededication of the Barbee monument and the slave auction block commemorative ceremony, two key events in this study.

The *PN&C* is widely read by local citizens and is considered to be an important text for the dissemination of community knowledge, including history. The paper contains information on local news, schools, the town government, crimes, births, deaths, and jobs. A section entitled "Yesteryears" highlights selected news stories from one hundred, fifty, and twenty-five years ago. Usually, historical photographs loaned by Page County citizens lie in the center. These photos are often of former or present residents in everyday settings. At the bottom of the page is a small space reserved for the column "Heritage and Heraldry" featuring historical stories written by prominent Valley historians.

Very often the history of German-Swiss settlement and the Confederacy is highlighted, reinforcing the hegemony of white male history here. Valley historians have also included stories of African American history, but these are few and far between, and on occasion, as will be seen in my work, presented with a slanted perspective. Nonetheless, the inclusion of history in a weekly paper reveals that local history is vital to people here.

Other primary collections included archival records on the Shenandoah National Park, promotional literature for Luray Caverns found in both the Page County Public Library and the Library of Congress, census records, and standing files in the library. I conducted approximately twenty-five interviews, both in person and on the Internet; visited businesses and spoke to their owners, sat in on town meetings and church services; and participated in preservation efforts by working with the preeminent history-making organization in town, the Page County Heritage Association (PCHA). Ethnography and oral history work were crucial to uncovering African American history because so little of this history is preserved by written sources.

In chapter one, I utilize these myriad primary sources to provide a historical overview of the history of Luray not in a one-dimensional, chronological way, but by combining a historical written narrative with an analysis of the public history sites that represent and symbolize elements of these narratives. I examine the two principal historical texts my white informants considered to be the most comprehensive sources on the history of the county since European settlement.[13] Through a close look, however, these works are tendentious narratives romanticizing the lifeways of the German-Swiss settlers to this area and the faithful service of the Confederate army. Consequently, since the late 1800s, public history sites have been devoted to these histories and have excluded commemoration of Native American and African American history. Both groups are relegated to stereotypes: Native Americans are savages, posing constant threats to the white settlers, and African American history is told through the discourse of slavery; it portrays enslaved African Americans as criminals, insurrectionists, and always overseen by benevolent white masters, often descendents of or actually founding white families to this area. In Luray, this "ruling class" comprises mostly descendents and/or long-time residents of Luray who, over the past one hundred years, have created commemorative landscapes that reflect a white, German-Swiss and Confederate past to the exclusion of Native Americans and African Americans. Thus, while Luray has resisted change from outsiders to create its own vision of the past, it has excluded minority populations from this vision.

I will also examine Luray as a town in the Shenandoah Valley, a distinctive region of the South, both similar and different to other areas, but a culture that emerged economically, geographically, and culturally apart from Appalachia and the rest of the South in terms of both white and Black history.

In this chapter I also look in depth at the first large-scale heritage celebration, the dedication of the Barbee Confederate Soldier statue in 1898. As part of a larger effort throughout the north and south to commemorate the Civil War dead, this event started heritage commemorations around the statue that continued even one hundred years later with the rededication of the Barbee monument in 1998. Both dedications, however, excluded the contributions of African Americans to the social and cultural fabric of life in the Shenandoah Valley during and after the Civil War. Indeed, after the war white southern democrats and other heritage organizations constructed commemorative landscapes devoted to Confederate heritage for political reasons, purposefully excluding African Americans.

In chapter two I continue to look at Luray's exclusionary narratives and landscapes, but also discuss how African Americans have been and continue to be vital players in Luray's history. An examination of the differences between how African American and white histories are told reveals inequitable treatment in historical narratives. But by closely investigating primary sources including a surviving slave narrative written by Bethany Veney, a slave born and raised in Page County who later became free, I assert that not only were African Americans contributing to the settlement and culture of the Shenandoah Valley, but also participating in a slave system based not on large plantations, but on smaller, more intimate farm communities. Thus, the physical landscape of the Shenandoah Valley may have created a distinctive form of slavery, one which is understudied, yet deserving of much more in-depth research.

Very early on in my ethnographic work, one of my informants told me about the most prominent African American public history site in Luray, the slave auction block. In chapter three, I outline the oral history of this block, the only type of history that exists. I include a discussion of how and why its story is discredited by white citizens and historians because it cannot be documented in printed fact, and because it threatens to undermine the southern, white hegemony of the public history here. Thus, the block is a subversive history site, sparking dialogues of race relations. While the practice of heritage is political and can be exclusive, in this instance it becomes one of the only ways African American history can be seen on the landscape.

As I began to investigate the history of the block and its role in the community for both whites and African Americans through critical ethnographic work, or, ethnography that asks critical questions of informants to create social change, I constantly tried to come to terms with my outsider status both in terms of my being white and not from the region. I was, from the beginning, asked what was I doing here and what did I want, mostly from my white informants. Also, I was not in Luray long before I noticed that the schism between white and African American landscapes and public history forced me to keep the information I gained separate from each race. My chief African American informant warned me about this identity hiding and revealing, a situation for which I was not prepared.[14]

While difficult and perhaps even dangerous in a racially-charged community, ethnographic work combined with cultural landscape study may be one of the only ways to expose African American history: there were several sites associated with African American history extant on the landscape (and mostly neglected) that I would never have known about had I not talked to individuals. Ethnography opened up the possibility that other structures on the landscape, particular to the African American community here, could be considered public history sites, especially churches—the first visual evidence of the African American community in Luray's landscape in the 1880s.

African American heritage celebrations in northern cities in the early nineteenth century were focused on the church, and in Luray, homecoming celebrations, also celebrated in the church are probably the most important expressions of heritage in the African American community. African American history deserves more presence on the landscape, but it also must be understood and examined in ways and methods separate from white history. Historians Genevieve Fabre and Robert O'Meally suggest that African American public history should be viewed in terms of *lieux de memoire*, or looking not just at museums and monuments, but at more diverse types of cultural expression.[15] Churches and homecoming celebrations can be included in this definition.

Just as public history definitions need to become more racially and ethnically inclusive, so too does tourism scholarship. In chapter four I trace the history of tourism of Luray, and look at the relationship between tourism and Luray's commemorative landscape. As I studied tourism within the community and through primary sources, I discovered that unlike other areas of Appalachia that have become commodified over the last century, Luray has managed to resist large-scale social and cultural change from tourism and asserted its own conceptions of heritage on the landscape. Instead, the history of tourism here reveals negotiation and cooperation between tourists and local citizens. Vituperative reactions towards any outsiders are reserved for the relatively recent influx of retirees who have moved from the Northern Virginia area to make their homes in Luray, the postmodern tourists.

A historic view of tourism also reveals the presence of African Americans as tourists in both Luray and the Shenandoah National Park in the early twentieth century. Through oral history work I was able to locate extant and non-extant structures that housed traveling African Americans in Luray. I was not successful, however, in finding much scholarly literature or critical theory on this topic. Forced to stay in rooms and spaces off the main roads, pack lunches and receptacles for human waste because they could not stop along the road, and finding places to stay from word-of-mouth and through written sources such as, *The Negro Motorist Green Book*, African Americans experienced tourism on a completely different and understudied level. African American tourism is a topic that needs further exploration as tourism becomes more important to scholars and to the global economy.

My final chapter looks at how a revised exhibition at the Shenandoah National Park's visitor center, only minutes from Luray, and a crucial part of Luray's history, is an engaging history display. This exhibition proves that critical and political public history can be done, and that a community's heritage can be recaptured. In 1966, as the Park Service attempted to create more hospitable visitor centers, it also tried to create an exhibition in the park which served its ideological goals—namely, to promote a patriotic and progressive view of America's history. This biased approach was especially damaging to the local community in the Shenandoah Valley as it justified the removal of culturally "backward" people for the construction of the Park. Today, wounds from the relocation project are still raw, but the new exhibition, done in conjunction with input from community members, proves that public history venues can exhibit critical views of the past, and federal organizations like the National Park Service are willing to undertake these important projects.

Presently, Luray's Main Street (and streets and communities all over the country) remain segregated and the slave auction block bears a new wreath recently placed on it by a white citizen, who wants it declared not as a piece of Black history, but as a carriage stepping stone. But White and African American history are inextricably intertwined. Our very quality of life is affected by how we see—or do not see ourselves in history and in the public history around us. It is my hope that this study will lead to more explorations of the role of heritage and history in our lives and to the myriad ways we can share our heritage on our commemorative landscapes.

NOTES

1. James W. Loewen, *Lies Across America: What Our Historic Sites Get Wrong* (New York: Free Press, 1999); David Lowenthal, *Possessed by the Past: The Heritage Crusade and the Spoils of History* (New York: Free Press, 1996).

2. David Lowenthal, *Possessed by the Past*, 121.

3. Lowenthal, *Possessed by the Past*, 63.
4. See Christopher Tilley and Michael Shanks, *Re-constructing Archeology* (New York: Routledge), 1992; Mark Leone and Neil Asher Silberman, eds. *Invisible America: Unearthing Our Hidden History* (New York: Henry Holt & Company, 1995).
5. Pierce Lewis, "Common Landscapes as Historic Documents," in *History From Things: Essays on Material Culture* (Washington, DC: Smithsonian Press, 1993), 115–39. I took Lewis's definition of cultural landscapes to help define the term commemorative landscapes.
6. D.W. Meinig, "The Beholding Eye: Ten Versions of the Same Scene," in *The Interpretation of Ordinary Landscapes: Geographical Essays*, D.W. Meinig, editor (New York: Oxford, 1979), 33–48.
7. Rhys Isaac, "Ethnographic Method in History: An Action Approach," in *Material Life in America: 1600–1860,* Robert Blair St. George, editor (Boston: Northeastern University Press, 1988), 39–61; Mary Corbin Sies, "Toward a Performance Theory of the Suburban Ideal, 1877–1917," in *Perspectives in Vernacular Architecture IV*, Thomas Carter and Bernard Herman, eds. (University of Missouri Press, 1991).
8. Kenneth E. Koons and Warren R. Hofstra, eds., *After the Backcountry: Rural Life in the Great Valley of Virginia, 1800–1900* (Knoxville: University of Tennessee Press, 2000), xviii.
9. Quetzil E. Castaneda, *In the Museum of Maya Culture: Touring Chichen Itza* (Minneapolis: Regents of the University of Minnesota, 1996).
10. Dona Brown, *Inventing New England: Regional Tourism in the Nineteenth Century* (Washington, DC: Smithsonian Institution Press, 1995), 134.
11. Brown, *Inventing*, 127.
12. The term "postmodern tourist" was coined by anthropologist Mark Leone.
13. Harry Strickler, *A Short History of Page County, Virginia* (Richmond: Dietz Press, 1952); John W. Wayland, *The German Elements of the Shenandoah Valley* (Published by author, 1907).
14. The names of my informants were changed to preserve and respect their anonymity.
15. Robert O'Meally and Genevieve Fabre, "Introduction" in *History and Memory in African-American Culture* (New York: Oxford University Press, 1994).

Chapter One

Creating the Past in Luray

Luray, Virginia is situated in northwestern Virginia, about one and three quarter hours from Washington, D.C. by car (figure 2). The area now known as Page County (of which Luray is the county seat) was first home to Native Americans who settled in large numbers in the Late Archaic period (2500–1000 B.C.). Later, Woodland Indians walked the Blue Ridge mountains, constructed burial grounds, and left behind a distinctive pottery-type— Keyser-Cord marked pots—until 1600 A.D. In the early to mid-eighteenth century, German-Swiss pioneers from southern Germany and the eastern Cantons of Switzerland settled in the Shenandoah Valley,[1] and other German-Swiss settlers traveled the Great Valley road from Pennsylvania to make their homes here.[2] Page County, first formed in 1831, is and was one of the smaller and less populated counties in the valley region of Virginia.

Like many other small towns, Luray boasts of generations of founding families. The same family names from the first settlements in the area in the eighteenth century are found in the county's current weekly newspaper, *The Page News & Courier (PN&C)*, businesses, and in phone books. Some of my informants whose ancestors settled in Luray showed me their families' artifacts that ranged from old books to a timber-framed barn dating to 1841.[3] Family lineage resonates so strongly that it determines, in large part, the public history in Luray; that is, many structures deemed important historically and found in the tourism literature are properties and monuments associated with the founding settlers to this area and Confederate ancestors.

This introductory chapter will tell Luray's story not in a linear fashion, but with a look at some of the public history sites that focus on a particular time period, event, or person. Since this is a cultural landscape and history study, the dialectical relationship between the landscape and historical texts needs to

11

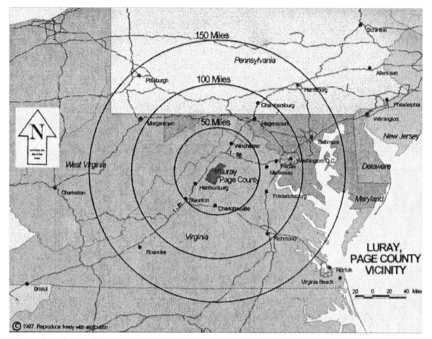

Figure 2.   Luray Map

be examined to reveal how the landscape reflects the history the town finds important. More succinctly, these narratives and sites are important to explore concomitantly since much of what is celebrated in the narratives is also celebrated on the landscape: A romanticized and nostalgic history focused on the struggles and the strong religious character of white, German-Swiss forefathers, and the sacrifices of ancestral Confederate soldiers. In order to maintain this commemorative hegemony, the history of Native Americans and especially African Americans is nearly absent. In Luray, white heritage functions as an ideological tool: the landscape only reflects the history of the descendents making it seem that they were the only individuals responsible for establishing the town and the county.

While mostly overlooked in history texts, Native Americans and African Americans actually do play parts, but their histories smack of sensationalism and myth: American Indians become murderous villains and threats to white settlement if they appear at all, and African Americans are virtually ignored since, as the early narratives and many of my white informants insisted, slavery was not a prominent fixture on the landscape of Page County and the Shenandoah Valley. Thus, the history reflected in the landscape is largely determined today by the preeminent heritage organization in Luray, the Page

County Heritage Association (PCHA). Most members of the PCHA have families with longstanding ties to the area; they are descendents of the revered German-Swiss and Confederate soldier forefathers. However, the images of industrious and religiously devoted early settlers and the self-sacrificing Confederate soldiers are created in the present to justify this heritage hegemony. The tourism literature, which used and still uses these primary historical texts, reinforces an exclusive landscape. Visitors and citizens alike are only exposed to bowdlerized versions of Luray's history.

The strength and vitality of the first Valley settlers, and the Confederate soldiers are interpretive threads running throughout written narratives, the commemorative landscape, and with many of my white informants. Over and over qualities of self-reliance, thrift, religious devotion, and strong family ties are reiterated in these texts, including the most comprehensive history on Page County, Harry Strickler's *A Short History of Page County, Virginia* (1952), considered by many of my informants to be the preeminent source on Luray and Page County history, and John Wayland's *The German Element of the Shenandoah Valley of Virginia* (1907) and *History of Rockingham County* (1912).[4] Consider this description of work and family life of the first settlers:

> As has already been remarked, the life of the early Germans was a busy and often a strenuous one. Work with the hands was taught as a virtue, and rigid economy was cultivated as a marked accomplishment. . . . And yet that life had a lighter and brighter as well as a darker and sterner side. Wants were few and easily satisfied. With the stimulating breath of God's great out-doors giving untaught vigor to heart and eye and limb, there was a healthy joy in living—just living. . . . Then, at all times, there was the warm home hearth, where the boys and girls were generally found in their few hours of leisure; and, best of all, love was there also, and bound the circle firm and close, though perhaps the word itself was not often spoken.[5]

Wayland, a descendent of Valley pioneers, and lifetime resident of nearby Rockingham County, creates a nostalgic and idealized picture of life that is found in the other historical narratives of the Valley.

If we look at the dates of publication for these historical works, especially Wayland's *The German Element of the Shenandoah Valley*, it may not be surprising that an agrarian, Anglo-Saxon German character was revered. During the late nineteenth–early twentieth centuries, ancestor worship and nativist sentiments ran high. As Michael Kammen states, ". . . Americans used 'ancestor worship' primarily to enhance the prestige of the living more than to honor the dead, and they pursued aspects of ancestor worship in order to marginalize or exclude less 'desireable' inhabitants."[6] Perhaps reacting to massive waves of immigrants at the turn of the century, and yearning for a simpler life, diametrically opposed to the Industrial Revolution, a distinctive Valley cultural identity was born. At this time as well, waves of nostalgia permeated the social fabric of America due to a civil war, industrialization, and, as Kammen asserts, ". . . a crumbling of a venerated value system, like religion."[7] Importantly, manifestations of nostalgia, like Strickler's and Wayland's works, were not necessarily driven by a desire to escape the present. Instead, they helped reinforce and legitimize current social and political structures so that these structures would serve as stabilizers in an unsettled, chaotic world. Frederic Jameson expands this definition and function of nostalgia by suggesting that idealization of specific periods, for example, the 1950s, as a time of the emergence of Beat poets and rock-and-roll, distorts the reality of the time. He argues that "period concepts finally correspond to no realities whatsoever," and ". . . the collective reality of the multitudinous lives encompassed by such terms is nonthinkable. . . ."[8] Nostalgia of this sort—of assigning social and cultural values and traits to a given period of time—distances the present from the past since the actual experience of historical actors may not match the concepts created for them.[9]

In creating their nostalgic picture of life in the Shenandoah Valley, both Wayland and Strickler also filled their works with copies of deeds received by the original settlers, census statistics, and court records. The inclusion of deeds also offers, in writing, proof of land ownership, but also the legitimate right of the earliest families to the land they were to settle. The forefathers, then, in a seemingly natural progression, have provided contemporary families with the same rights to land and settlement, and thus, preeminence in historical narratives and the landscape. This ownership of the land also justifies, however, the removal of other populations who were actually the very first inhabitants, the American Indians. Not only were they not entitled to land, but they impeded the progress of white people by being constant and dangerous menaces to them.

The early settlers, in addition to laying the foundation for an agrarian culture, are perceived, nostalgically, as religiously devout, and the ubiquity of churches and meeting houses devoted to them is reflected on the landscape. Lutherans and Mennonites, and later, Baptists and Methodists and members of the Church of the Brethren, left their mark on the county's landscape through the construction of churches. The congregations of Mt. Calvary and St. Peter's Lutheran churches are two of Page County's oldest "continuously meeting groups," dating from the 1730s.[10] Mt. Calvary, having been renovated, still stands today in the Stony Man area of Luray. St. Peter's is located in the town of Shenandoah in Page County.

Baptists and Mennonites together formed the Mill Creek Church, or the Mauck Meeting House, an important structure maintained by the Page County

Heritage Association (PCHA) and listed consistently in the main historical narratives of Page County and tourism literature. Dating from 1772 and located in Hamburg, two miles west of Luray on U.S. 211, the church reflects a unique architectural form with the entrance on the non-gable side. Most of the other churches in Luray and the county possess a standard nave-plan form with entry on the gable end and the pulpit opposite the gable end.[11]

The austere Mauck Meeting House embodies the simple, yet strong faith of the early settlers, and it also serves as an important location for a heritage event—the annual Christmas concert sponsored by the PCHA. Local choirs and individuals perform to an audience comprised mostly of PCHA members, as I noticed after attending the event for two years in 1999 and 2000. Although many popular Christmas songs are sung, a strong religious component exists. As a public history site, Mauck both commemorates the religious devotion of the German settlers, and provides a venue for community expressions of faith. For the last two years, as well, an African American gospel choir was invited to sing, the first time the PCHA has involved members of the African American community to participate. I will return to this event in chapter two.

In 1929, the Massanutten Monument was erected, located five miles west of Luray and dedicated to the founders of this settlement in 1729. Its bronze tablet reads, "To the founders of the Massanutten settlement. . . . For their foresight, courage, industry, and moral worth. . . ." Usually found in tourist and traveler brochures and guidebooks, it is quite a distance from downtown Luray. This obelisk or chimney-style monument made of large stones is a public history site that glorifies the honorable and religiously devout German settlers, implying that they were inherently industrious and kind.

Figure 3. Massanutten Monument

This untainted ethnic character is discussed in *Page: County of Plenty*, a short book written for the nation's bicentennial, and considered to be one of the essential histories of the county. This work, like Strickler's and Wayland's, argues that these early settlers were victims of inauspicious economic and social conditions and the English Colonial government. For example, Jacob Stover, considered the most influential first settler as he was the patentee of the Massanutten settlement, gained the reputation through "various histories" of being an "unscrupulous land agent."[12] But *Page: County of Plenty* dismisses this accusation by insisting that he was "a victim of knavish government officials" and, provocatively, was an ancestor of President Dwight D. Eisenhower, further glorifying his character.[13]

The most prodigious threat to the settlers was Native Americans who had roamed the Shenandoah Valley for thousands of years before white settlement. When the first white people explored the region in the mid-seventeenth century, the area that is now the Shenandoah National Park was populated by Sioux-speaking groups, with "about one thousand Manahoac and a similar scattering of Monocan."[14] By 1700, according to Valley historian Darwin Lambert, most American Indians had died from smallpox, measles, and tuberculosis, diseases brought by whites, or had moved out of the area.[15] Arrowheads, pottery, pipes, and other artifacts attest to the presence of American Indians, as do historical narratives, like Wayland's and Strickler's.

In nearly all of these works, American Indians are relegated to murdering marauders and nuisances to the white pioneers. For example, the various Massanutten settlement forts, Fort Egypt, and Fort Roads, remarkable for, among other reasons, the presence of vaulted cellars, are described as defensive structures (hence the title "Fort").[16] While it is possible that loopholes in the cellars were used to attack aggressive American Indians, they were principally designed to store perishable food. While remarkable vestiges of a distinctive vernacular architectural style, the forts are renowned only for their roles as fortifications against hostile American Indians.

In 1764, Fort Roads, for example, was the site of a massacre in which a Mennonite minister and pacifist (John Roads) and his family were murdered. One son was taken away as a prisoner.[17] These stories, embellished with sensationalism, frame how indigenous peoples are perceived in narratives and in tourism literature, where these sites are also mentioned. Even in the recently published *Touring the Shenandoah Valley Backroads*, a visitor's guide to various sections of the Valley, the story of John Roads is included:

> The attackers shot and killed the reverend and his wife immediately. They also brutally murdered several of the couple's children. One of the family's older daughters grabbed her toddler sister and escaped by running to safety at a neighbor's house. One son was kidnapped by the Indians but managed to return to the Valley about three years later. The attackers never found the money, which was stashed in a cellar wall, so they set the home on fire before they left.[18]

These stories of American Indian aggression and attack versus white settler innocence cloud historical truths and reinforce cultural and ethnic stereotypes. Clearly, Indian massacres were violent and tragic events, and, in the case of the Roads tragedy, it is his family who were truly victims. But comprehensive research reveals that American Indian and white violence were based on historical realities. For example, the fur trade that began in the late seventeenth century ignited bloodshed in the Iroquois Confederacy that was supported by Dutch and English settlers. According to National Park historian Reed Engle and writer Hugh Crandall, "these tribes spread warfare south in their attempt to monopolize the lucrative fur trade."[19] Thus, while American Indians are characterized as inherently drawn to violence and attacking whites, research reveals that the profit-driven fur trade also played a part in this bloodshed. Moreover, the fur trade proved fatal to the American Indian way of life in the Valley. Dreams and realities of profits made from the fur trade not only exploited land and natural resources, but brought indigenous peoples into the race for profit. Simultaneously, the desire for land, prompted by the prosperous and powerful Alexander Spotswood, governor of the Virginia Colony, led him and a team of explorers to cross the Blue Ridge Mountains in 1716, opening the Valley to white settlement.

The "Knights of the Golden Horseshoe" monument, named for Spotswood's men and the golden horseshoe he apparently gave each of them for their loyalty and bravery, commemorates the crossing of the Blue Ridge by Alexander and stands as testament to westward expansion. The approximately six feet high stone pyramid rests at Swift Run Gap, near one of the entrances to the Shenandoah National Park, in Greene County. But since the monument was sponsored and erected by the Colonial Dames of Virginia in 1921—a time when white filiopeitic groups were burgeoning—it also stands as a symbol of the glorification of colonial history, and the hegemony of white history.

Modern debates about whether or not Spotswood and his team actually crossed the Blue Ridge at Swift Run Gap are raging. In April 2001, an amateur historian from Luray, Tom Sites, organized a debate around this issue.[20] He suggests that the expedition records are muddled and confusing because of a French Huguenot's account of the team drinking excessively. Further, Sites feels that this historical episode has been tainted by romanticism beginning in the 1800s and continuing today.[21]

As the English gentry fought over land boundaries and rights, the Indian problem became less of an issue. Each new county in Virginia formed militias to quell Indian troublemakers.[22] Historian Darwin Lambert quotes a prominent Virginian during the peak English settlement years:

I confess my feelings are hurt and my humanity shocked by the unbounded thirst of our people after Lands that they cannot cultivate, and the means they use to possess themselves of those that belong to others. An Indian has his National rights as well as a White man.[23]

Ironically, while American Indian names, including Shenandoah, Massanutten, and Stony Man Mountain pervade maps, popular, and historical literature, an extensive, historically accurate account of the earliest inhabitants is very hard to find in books, and nearly impossible on the commemorative landscape. At the John Roads house, a memorial exists only to the massacred whites. Even today, the American Indians in this area are remembered as aggressors and threats to white settlement. In a recent column of the *PN&C,* the story of Mary Draper Ingles, taken captive by the Shawnees, is reported, with Ingles's heroism the center of the story.[24]

The early settlers cultivated corn, wheat, tobacco, and hemp, and took advantage of their proximity to the Shenandoah River to transport these goods.[25] New trade routes to eastern Virginia, including the Tidewater area, enabled early farmers to market their goods beyond the immediate confines of the county. Slaves may also have been traded along these routes, and communication lines were established for the "borrowing" of slaves who worked in the iron works and other industries.[26]

Industries needed to support farm production, including tanning, millstone manufacturing, and blacksmithing, sprung up in the county in the early eighteenth century. The abundance of iron deposits in the surrounding mountains generated other employment possibilities. Catherine Furnace, dating to 1836, was an important site, reported to have supplied shells for the Mexican and Civil Wars. It is listed on the Virginia Historic Landmark Register and the National Register of Historic Places. The Shenandoah Iron Works (SIW), founded in 1836, was one of the most successful iron businesses in antebellum Virginia at this time.[27] Slaves as well as free blacks worked these furnaces along with whites.

In tourist literature, and in the county's historical accounts, the furnaces are important because they were used to support the Confederacy. Iron from Catherine Furnace, for example, was shipped to Richmond, Virginia, and iron pigs supplied the gun works at Harper's Ferry, West Virginia.[28] No source on this site mentions the workers at these furnaces, and that some, if not many, were African Americans, a subject of the next chapter.

By 1830, Luray, Stanley, and Shenandoah were expanding commercially and architecturally, and in 1831 Page County was formed. Trade had begun with the east, hotels and government buildings were erected, and stores were built, showing that an era of consumption hit Page County. The Page County Courthouse, of Jeffersonian Classical design and completed in 1833, reveals that this area was following the architectural trends of the east.[29]

The history of the Civil War in Page County and Luray is complex, well documented, and a popular subject for local historians and scholars. Volunteer companies were formed and there were some engagements, but no major battles took place in the county. Perhaps the best-known "episode" of the War was named, morbidly, "The Burning." In 1864, General Philip H. Sheridan "resolved to destroy the Valley's agricultural potential and thereby cripple the Southern war effort."[30] Sheridan's actions were devastating: many barns and mills were destroyed. Union soldiers burned acres of farmland and the isolation of the town hindered economic recovery. Page County also suffered from the lack of able-bodied men to help sustain industry. In 1864, the Page County Court sent a petition to the Confederate government to turn over men who were blacksmiths, wagon makers, and involved in similar industries to the war effort. It stated: "We are now unable to have the limited quantities of grain that has been left us converted into meal and wholly unable to have such mill work as is absolutely necessary to have done."[31]

As part of Reconstruction efforts, northern capitalists, or carpetbaggers, seeing the opportunity for profit and exploiting labor, offered Page County citizens the chance to recoup their losses through the construction of a railroad.[32]

Money was pledged for bonds, but the sponsoring company ran out of money and the project was put on hold until the late nineteenth century. This depot is now in the midst of massive renovations and will be an important heritage and tourist destination for Luray.

The Civil War's legacy is found in the commemorative landscapes in Luray and in many towns throughout the Shenandoah Valley. The Southern Cross flag flies from homes and shops, and Civil War Trails Markers are found on major and lesser-known roads, honoring battles, skirmishes, or historical figures.

In Luray, near the center of town, at the intersection of Main Street and Reservoir Road, stands the Confederate soldier monument—the single most important piece of public history for the white citizens of Luray. Sculpted by Herbert Barbee, a Luray native, the Barbee

Figure 4.   Confederate Statue

Confederate statue (as it is now called) was dedicated with much fanfare in July 1898 (figure 4). A special ceremony involved a group of women carrying flags of the twelve Southern States which contributed funds to Barbee because he had trouble raising the money himself. Barbee, who lived in Calendine, the site of PCHA's museum and a noted tourist destination, is probably the most revered figure in Luray's history. His motivation for creating the statue began with a visit to Gettysburg, where he noticed the plethora of monuments dedicated to the fallen Northern soldiers. He stated in a newspaper interview:

> Passing over the famous battlefield of Gettysburg some years ago, and recounting the valiant deeds of the two contending armies, I counted nearly five hundred monuments reared as just tributes to Northern heroism, and in the midst of this lavish display of art, wealth, beauty, grace and taste, seeing but one simple stone marking the death spot of a Confederate soldier, I turned from this once bloody field where my sentiments had fallen, with a resolve to return to my native town—Luray, Page county—and there build a fitting tribute to their honor . . . yet I would that we should not lose our reverence and veneration for those whose faithfulness and heroism of the past is now a part of our common history and heritage.[33]

Today the statue remains a symbol of the personal sacrifices the individual men gave for the South. Similarly, the rededication, occurring in July 1998, one hundred years later, was also a significant event in the town's history. One of my informants, a member of PCHA, commented that the rededication was "the biggest thing we've ever done."[34] The Luray Chapter of the United Daughters of the Confederacy helped support this event, where nearly 2,000 people attended, and other town organizations provided in-kind services. In addition to dedication ceremonies, activities included a parade, a Civil War living history exhibit, the selling of Confederate military memorabilia, and refreshments. The celebration featured songs pertinent to Confederate history, including "The Bonnie Blue Flag," the controversial "Carry Me Back to Ol' Virginia," originally Virginia's state song, but removed in the 1990s for racist language, and the Confederate anthem, "Dixie." One of my informants stated, ". . . my views as both a UDC member and personally are one and the same. More than 1900 Page County men marched off to war. Some did not return. A marble statue to honor them is the least we could do. . . . I'm glad there are two."[35] Another informant told me what the dedication to the Barbee monument meant to her:

> Been thinking about the questions you asked me: "Do you have personal feelings toward one or the other?" concerning the two Confederate monuments that we have in Luray. Not really. I participated in the parade we had for the rededication, and I admit that I felt a sense of pride in being the descendant of a Confederate

soldier. I also was thinking that my grandparents and my great-grandparents were actually present at the original dedication, and here I was 100 years later being a part of the rededication.[36]

In fact, the strong sentiments toward the Barbee statue are related to the erection of a second Confederate memorial, located near the intersection of Route 340 and Main Street. According to some Luray citizens, the second soldier, a more ornate monument, was erected in 1917 because the Barbee monument soldier was dressed too shabbily. Another informant told me the Barbee soldier is not facing "defiantly north" and is considered unacceptable. He claimed that Barbee's prurient, scandalous reputation tainted the monument so a more pure Confederate, then, was needed.[37] Yet another informant felt that the second monument was desired because the Barbee monument was "too far out in the country at the time it was erected."[38]

Herbert Barbee, of course, as creator of the soldier monument, is a renowned historical figure in the town, and his home, Calendine, across the street from the Mauck Meeting House, is a historic house museum. As revered as Barbee is, however, oral interviews shed a more controversial light on the artist. One of my informants remarked that Barbee was somewhat of an eccentric because of his devotion to sculpting nudes:

I've heard that some people didn't like Mr. Barbee, the one who carved the statue at this site [points to where Barbee statue is located] because he was an artist and he was a little more advanced back in the 1860s, and he used to carve nudes, and you can imagine how some of these old farmers and everything, you know, thought about that and it was just scandalous. So they probably thought he was desecrating the Confederate soldier—that he was some sinner.[39]

Since the Barbee monument was considered too far on the outskirts of town, created by a scandalous, free-thinking artist, and not facing due north, another monument was built in the center of town.

The grand celebration in Luray was replicated in many areas of both the North and the South in the post-Civil War years, fueling a monument movement unseen in American history. Although monuments and memorials existed before the Civil War, it was only after the war that a movement to commemorate the common soldier in sculptural form took hold. Supported in large part by the federal government, but also by state and regional interests, and a new burgeoning monument industry, commemoration reached new heights literally and figuratively. According to G. Kurt Piehler, the advent of photographic images and a novel perspective on individual soldiers sparked these new forms of public memory.[40]

Kirk Savage also explores public commemoration and race in the post-Civil War years. Savage, however, offers a divergent argument to the phenomenon of the citizen-soldier form in the monument movement. He asserts that the Civil War was unprecedented in terms of loss of life, and the first time "a mass army of volunteers had to endure the reality of prolonged life as soldiers."[41] The savagery of warfare led, Savage believes, to a devastating identity crisis for men, with "a drastic curtailing of personal agency and a concomitant loss of 'manhood.'"[42] Thus, monuments devoted to a single soldier were designed to help men regain masculine pride, and a society to heal from the debilitating effects of war.

The new soldier monuments also transformed the way war was symbolized, and set the tone for how heritage groups commemorate war. With organizations such as the Daughters of the American Revolution, Sons of Confederate Veterans, the United Daughters of the Confederacy, and many other similar groups emerging in the last decade of the nineteenth century, heritage became linked to lineage, upon connection to individual ancestors.[43] In my interviews, my white informants often described individual soldiers and struggles (usually their ancestors) when I asked them about their history, showing that this type of commemoration is still prevalent today. In May 2001, the United Daughters and Sons of the Confederacy sponsored a "lumination" ceremony at the site of the second Confederate memorial (which will be discussed below), where one candle was lit for each casualty, reinforcing the importance of the memory of individual soldiers.

In July 1917, Luray ordered a new Confederate monument from the McNeel Marble Company in Marietta, Georgia, signifying that a commercial enterprise was capable of creating a symbolically-charged marker of Confederate memory (figure 5). The *PN&C* described the monument as follows:

> The soldier figure will be of Imported Italian marble and the rest of the structure will be silver gray Georgia marble, quarried at Marietta, GA. The McNeel Marble Company which is to furnish this monument has erected 75 per cent. of all the Confederate Monuments erected in the South. This company owns its own quarres [sic], employs its own sculptors and is equipped with the latest and most expensive machinery for turning out monuments, insuring perfect workmanship and is a guarantee against unsightly mortar joints that appear in monuments not properly constructed.[44]

Named the Broad Street Confederate Monument, it cost a hefty $3,000 to erect and thousands of citizens came out to celebrate its dedication. Manufactured monuments, then, retained artistic integrity and could publicly represent Confederate soldier and war memory.

Monument making was big business in the late nineteenth and early years of the twentieth century throughout the country, and consumers were willing

Confederate Monument to be erected at Luray, Va.
MONUMENT COMMITTEE
W. McKim, Chairman   Fred T. Amiss, Sec. & Treas.

Figure 5.   2nd Confederate Statue

to accept these assembly-line public monuments.[45] Efforts to commemorate the Civil War were undertaken on local levels, but the impetus for commemoration was very much a national movement. Tied inextricably into postwar politics, commemorative activities in the South were overseen by elite white community members, most often descendents of revolutionary and colonial era families. This population, largely consisting of members of the Democratic party, sought to overcome the humiliation of defeat and reassert their ancestry and dominance in town and national politics. The erection of public monuments devoted to the glory of the Lost Cause, was one method of regaining pride and cultural identity:

In the 1880s and early 1890s, patrician Democrats began to call for a rehabilitation of state and southern history and the erection of civic monuments dedicated to that history, transforming the cult of defeat into the dominant culture of power regained. At the end of the century, the turbulent political campaigns of 1898 and 1900 riveted public attention and generated new themes in the Democrats' use of history. After 1900 the reentrenched elite turned with unprecedented energy and conviction to the shaping of public memory and the creation of official symbols, which quickly established a codified tradition and transformed the setting of public life.[46]

In reclaiming physically damaged landscapes and erecting monuments as evidence of renewal, the Democrats also sought to maintain white power in defiance of the emancipation of slaves. As Anglo-Saxon supremacy dominated the landscape, no room was left for telling the history of those who were not white. Excluded, then, from the commemorative landscape and a place in Reconstruction politics, African Americans were continually subjugated. Perhaps this subjugation was most evident in the formation of the Ku Klux Klan in 1866. Further, white southerners openly resisted efforts by the federal government to grant southern African Americans political and economic rights.[47]

The thousands of African Americans who participated in the war were not a part of the burgeoning public commemoration of the citizen soldier. In post-Civil War America, the service of African Americans was not a part of the new surges of nationalistic pride. In fact, Savage goes so far as to argue that the monuments, solely devoted to the white soldier, served as ideological symbols of racism:

> . . . in the public sphere the creation and recreation of whiteness is inseparable from the creation and recreation of blackness. The marginalization of African America went hand in hand with the reconstruction of white America. African Americans could not be included *or* excluded in the landscape of public sculpture without changing the fabric of commemoration itself, without ultimately changing the face of the nation.[48]

Forced to the periphery, African Americans were commemorated publicly only as slaves, as supporters of the white man. One of the only mentions of African Americans participating in a public history event in Luray occurs in a commemorative booklet on the event of the Barbee statue dedication in 1898. One of the floats in the procession before the unveiling held a vivid tableau vivant:

> A feeling of reverence and sacredness, mingled with admiration, was felt, as the float, representing the burial of Lantane, a Confederate soldier killed in battle, passed. On it were a coffin, two stalwart negroes with shovels, and two little girls, in the act of strewing flowers.[49]

The tableau vivant, a popular form of entertainment in which individuals wore costumes and posed motionless to replicate art, history, or literature, found its largest audience in the late 1800s. Although a form of parlor entertainment, the displays also found an audience during local parade and civic celebrations, literally freezing the art, history, or literary figure or scene a community deemed important, in time. Notably, in this Luray celebration, the subservient role of gravediggers—a role relegated to many African Americans in the Civil War—fits the fantasy atmosphere of a Lost Cause.

Not all African Americans willingly participated in historic displays as slaves. In 1889, a group of African American residents in Philadelphia refused to participate in a tableau honoring the Centennial of the Constitution that would have had them stand as symbols of slavery.[50] Thus, in Luray, as well as hundreds of towns throughout the country after Reconstruction, commemorative sculpture devoted to the Civil War and civic celebrations contained strikingly racist elements: public history centered on the struggles and stories of whites obfuscated the significant role of African Americans in the war and, conversely, placed them in scenarios of servitude with a romanticized perspective.

Confederate memory has also spawned various heritage groups in town including the United Daughters of the Confederacy, Sons of Confederate Veterans, and the Page County Genealogical Society. To become a member of the UDC or SCV, one must prove bloodlines to Confederate ancestors, and certainly since African Americans were not allowed to serve in the Confederacy as soldiers, their inclusion in these groups is impossible. Based on my interviews on these heritage events, the ideology at work here is that only white, southern manhood is worthy of historical preservation and heritage celebration for these groups—a one-dimensional, single perspective on the history of the town.

The arrival of the railroad in the late 1800s forever changed life in Page County and in the Shenandoah Valley. No longer having to rely on flatboats or barges to transport goods, the citizens constructed a depot in 1907, which established a base for economic growth and tourism. The depot also became the gathering site of thousands of turn-of-the-century elite tourists en route to "Excursion Days" to the Luray Caverns, the ornate Queen Anne Hotel, the Luray Inn, or Skyland, a plush Victorian resort in the Blue Ridge Mountains that surround Luray.[51]

The iron furnace industry continued to flourish at this time, certainly also a result of railroad expansion. The construction of tanneries and mills—now operated by steam or gasoline—and canneries diversified the county's economy.[52] It was at this time, near the turn of the century, that the store at Hamburg, another major renovation project sponsored by the PCHA, was built.

After 1870, public schools for both white and African American citizens began to dot the landscape. Most of these schools were either one- or two-room structures, and of frame construction.[53] In the late 1800s, larger brick buildings housed students, including the Luray Graded and High School, located near the town office off of Main Street. The one-room Massanutten School, a noted historical and tourist site, is overseen by the PCHA. Moved from its original Massanutten location, it now stands prominently next to the library, the slave auction block, and the train depot. Many local students tour this school during the school year.

A similar one-room schoolhouse also exists in Hamburg, just off U.S. Highway 211—the Hamburg Colored School. Covered in vines and built in 1888, this school is not listed in the tourism literature of the town, although many of my informants, both white and African American, knew about it. One white informant expressed interest in moving the school or renovating it, but doubted the outcome would be favorable since the property on which the school lies is family-owned, with members of the family at odds with each other.[54]

Figure 6.   Massanutten School

A comparison of the two schoolhouses, one in disrepair and the other standing conspicuously right off Main Street bearing a historical marker, is striking
and represents, in a nutshell, the disparate treatments of African American public history and white history: White history is worthy of remembering and celebrating and African American history is not (figures 6 and 7). Moreover, the

Figure 7.　Black School

white school is equipped with desks and a cast-iron stove, designed to conjure up nostalgia for a simpler time. Is it possible that sentimentalized views of the past, often found in physical structures like one-room schoolhouses and colonial villages, are only possible or allowable with white history? If so, why? Is it impossible to look back at African American history nostalgically? Certainly the legacy of slavery, which is an essential part of the African American experience in Luray and in the United States is not an uplifting, positive history. Most importantly, perhaps, slavery is not just about the past: racial politics and tensions continue to resonate in the present, making the subject very difficult to represent. In 1994, for example, folklorist John Vlach curated the exhibit, "Back of the Big House: The Cultural Landscape of the Plantation," for the Library of Congress. Designed to show how enslaved African Americans were able to create and sustain cultural and social space despite the brutality of slavery, the exhibit was taken down three hours after it opened. According to African American employees of the Library, slavery was not over, and they did not want to be reminded of it.[55] Further, some African American staff members were embroiled in a dispute at that time over racial discrimination. Some staff referred to the administrative offices as "The Big House" and remarked that they were working on a "plantation."[56]

Combined with one-dimensional treatments in textbooks in school, a prevailing southern regional ideology that the Civil War was not about slavery, and a nationwide unsettled racial climate, representing slavery to the public remains challenging for public historians and even for individuals.[57] In Luray, the purported slave auction block, on the cusp of receiving a storyboard dedication and presently bearing a wreath dedicated to enslaved African Americans, is creating tension within the community. In chapter three I will look at how this piece of public history, which represents the past, is causing controversy in the present.

Throughout the twentieth century, and after the tourist lull during the post-World War II years, Luray benefited economically and culturally from an influx of visitors, and continued to celebrate heritage events, ranging from the dedication of a stadium to men "who gave their lives to World Wars I and II" in 1951 to a celebration of the opening of the train depot.[58] The Luray train depot, which opened in 1908, plays a very significant role in Luray's history and stands on the edge of major renovation. The PCHA, the Page County Railroad Club, the town government, and the newly formed Luray Train Station Restoration Alliance have all worked together to set in motion the first steps toward restoration. At present, the president of PCHA has commented that the depot will be restored to the period of the 1940s, a time yielding many photographs, especially of soldiers going off to war.[59] The depot will serve mainly as a visitor's center, a research and archival reading room overseen by the PCHA, exhibition space, and an office for the Luray-Page County Chamber of Commerce.[60]

The establishment of the Shenandoah National Park in 1935 was one of the most significant events to occur in Luray's history. In fact, as part of the celebration of the new millennium, the *PN&C* printed a special edition in which the "Story of the Century" was the construction of the Park.[61] The tourist cabins, hotels, shops, the Skyline Drive which stretches 105 miles north-south through the Park, and even government-built homes designed for people displaced by the Park, all changed Luray's landscape and economy. The Park and its controversial history as well as its effects on Luray and tourism will be discussed later in this work.

During the late 1960s and 1970s, new efforts were undertaken to create heritage associations and capture local history in time for the country's bicentennial.

The Page County Heritage Association (PCHA), established in 1969, became the preeminent history-making organization in Luray and in Page County. It maintains historic properties, and sponsors an annual Heritage Festival, as well as other events throughout the year, and is comprised mostly of Luray and Page County natives. The PCHA's mission is four-fold:

1. To foster the restoration and preservation of the historical and cultural heritage of Page County.
2. To make known, places, structures, scenic views, events and others as pertaining to the historical and cultural background and history of Page County.

3. To foster, plan and hold a Page County Festival for the purpose of exhibiting the arts and crafts and other exhibits of historical and cultural value as pertaining to Page County.
4. To acquire, own, and maintain property associated with the historical and cultural background and history of Page County.[62]

PCHA owns and maintains several historic structures already discussed in this chapter including Calendine, the antebellum home of famed sculptor Herbert Barbee, the Massanutten School, Mauck Meeting House, and the Hamburg store, a late-nineteenth century building, currently being renovated to its 1940s façade and interior. All of these properties are open to the public on a limited schedule and are run by volunteers. The School is the only historic site located in the center of Luray; Mauck, Calendine, and the Hamburg store are all a couple of miles outside of town on Highway 211. PCHA also holds membership meetings in other notable historic structures in the county, such as the churches mentioned earlier in this chapter.

Preceding the historic house museum at Calendine, the Luray Museum stood on Main Street, and for seventy years it drew visitors "from all over the world."[63] The Museum, which contained a plethora of artifacts such as war and Indian relics and jewelry, was founded circa 1890 around the acquisition of a single thing: a souvenir boot of Tom Thumb's. According to a historical account, a 12-year-old Valley resident went to see P.T. Barnum's show featuring Thumb. When she was invited on stage, she was given the boot. In 1960, the Luray Museum closed and its collection was sold at auction.[64]

While PCHA's historic sites host visitors, locals, and nearby students, their annual festival, held every year in October, is the main draw for most people, and the event that brings in a substantial amount of money to support other preservation and interpretive efforts. The two-day event features craft sellers and demonstrators, the Antique Tractor Steam and Gas Engine Show, a Civil War encampment, food, an "ole time" auction, an apple butter boiling (considered a culturally significant social event to the people of the Blue Ridge), musical shows with folk and bluegrass music, line dancing and cloggers, and an open house at all of PCHA's historic properties.

The items for sale and the celebration of heritage at the festival are a controlled display of culture, planned exclusively by PCHA's board. Although some tourism scholars have decried these celebrations as arenas of cultural commodification, this event is not a festival for outsiders necessarily, and it is not a display of cultural identity transformed and molded to fit outsider expectations. According to an informant:

> The Heritage Festival here . . . you want to generate income from the rentals of the stalls for the Festival, but on the other hand, you'd like for something that

the crafter has that is thematically compatible with the Heritage Festival. And the exhibits and the displays are not gimmicky, they're sorta genuine. . . . And now this entity [PCHA] is reaching a crossroads. There are new opportunities for expansion and greater recognition, a larger income generator and other activities. Preservation efforts as a result of appropriated income.[65]

The festival is serious business and serious heritage. Even though PCHA has experienced considerable growth with the festival, the guidelines for running the event, especially the restriction that all crafts for sale have to be handmade, remain stringent. Thus, the festival is an example of a heritage event that breaks the mold of scholarly conceptions of local celebrations performed to suit the desires and expectations of outsiders. In this event, most of the tourists are from other counties, not middle and upper class consumers from urban areas. Therefore, Dean MacCannell's claim that ". . . tourism promotes the restoration, preservation, and fictional recreation of ethnic attributes" needs to be questioned.[66] In simpler terms, perhaps, tourism scholarship needs to explore a more nuanced view of the power relations inherent in tourism and cultural displays, a subject taken up in chapter four of this work.

The festival is a celebration of heritage with the purpose of raising money to support the preservation and interpretative goals of the PCHA, but it is a celebration of *white* heritage, not the entire county's heritage. One of my informants, a member of a citizen's group devoted to racial equality in Luray, wanted to racially integrate this event and asked if her group could sponsor an exhibition on Luray's African American churches. She was refused:

It was funny because last year they had their heritage festival that they have every year and I had noticed that we never had anything about Black heritage, and so when we started meeting I said you know I think we ought to approach the Heritage Association and see if we can't have a booth or something; maybe we could have the history of the Black churches. This is a logical place to start— they've got all these photographs, they've got all this stuff. So it would be less labor-intensive, and we thought this was a really good idea, so I called [a member of PCHA] and I know him, and he thought that was fine. He put me in touch with a woman who is actually in charge of it [the festival] and she turned me down flat . . . and I went to talk to her and she said well we don't, it was so funny, she said, we don't have that kind of thing. But if you all have something you want to sell, and I said no, I said I've been to that before and I know there are historical displays and we would just like to have a table where we could put up a display on the history of the black churches. She said we don't do things like that. . . . This is a fundraiser for us.[67]

The festival *is* a fundraiser with exhibitors required to pay a percentage of what they make to the PCHA, and PCHA itself sells books. But PCHA also displays its current and future heritage projects and welcomes the heritage displays of Appalachian music, and steam and gas demonstrations, which are not money-making activities. Possibly, had my informant told the PCHA member that she had goods to sell associated with African American history, they would have been included in the festival. This idea, however, was not mentioned by the PCHA member and the festival remains devoted to celebrations of white heritage only.

In Luray, then, history and public displays of history are racially exclusive and focus on heroic ancestors and familial and communal lineage. This emphasis on nostalgia and genealogy, while vital to cultural identity, can cloud an accurate history for the public. Genealogy, as theorized by Michel Foucault, sets up history systemically and cleanly and falsely advertises that history and historical ancestry follow a natural path to the present. In the case of white genealogical groups, any contact is incidental and not important to the outcome of white supremacy on the commemorative landscape. History lies not in prefabricated, isolated, and determined paths, but what is found in between, what has been pushed to the margins. He writes:

> Genealogy does not pretend to go back in time to restore an unbroken continuity that operates beyond the dispersion of forgotten things; its duty is not to demonstrate that the past actively exists in the present, that it continues secretly to animate the present, having imposed a predetermined form to all its vicissitudes. Genealogy does not resemble the evolution of a species and does not map the destiny of a people. On the contrary, to follow the complex course of descent is to maintain passing events in their proper dispersion; it is to identify the accidents, the minute deviations—or conversely, the complete reversals—the errors, the false appraisals, and the faulty calculations that gave birth to those things that continue to exist and have value for us; it is to discover that truth or being do not lie at the root of what we know and what we are, but the exteriority of accidents.[68]

If accidents are the source of history, public history in Luray only reflects what seems to be the certainties—the rightful expansion of settlement by the German-Swiss, and the belief that Confederate soldiers are the only historical actors worth commemorating. Genealogy, as practiced in Luray, is vital and meaningful on personal, familial, and community levels, and serves as a source of heritage and pride for the town's citizens. The historical narratives and public history sites, focused on European settlement and the Confederacy, reveal that these genealogies are critical to sustaining and exhibiting a certain cultural identity. At the same time, however, genealogy, like nostalgia, can falsely glorify the past so that it becomes a predictable, heroic, mythic, and exclusive story. Genealogy and nostalgia become ideological tools, eliminating the possibility that any other cultures impacted the town's history and landscapes.

In November 2000, Willow Grove Mill in Luray received a new Civil War Trail marker noting its historic role: barns and homes were burned here in Sheridan's path of destruction. And although this area was also noted as the home and shop of Yancy Coleman, an African American blacksmith and "wonderful old ex-slave," his history is not mentioned in this site's marker.[69] Fortunately, records of African Americans in Luray and in the Shenandoah Valley do exist, and translate into a shared history. But, as we will see in the next chapter, this history does not translate into a shared heritage.

NOTES

1. *Page: The County of Plenty* (Page County: Page County Bicentennial Commission, 1976), 11.

2. Charles C. Ballard, *Dismissing the Peculiar Institution: Assessing Slavery in Page and Rockingham Counties, Virginia* (Luray: Page County Heritage Association, 1999), 1.

3. Pezzoni and Giles, 13.

4. Rockingham County lies immediately east of Page County, just over the Blue Ridge Mountains.

5. John Wayland, *The German Element of the Shenandoah Valley* (published by author, 1907), 201.

6. Michael Kammen, *Mystic Chords of Memory* (New York: First Vintage, 1991), 222.

7. Kamen, 195.

8. Frederic Jameson, *Postmodernism, or, the Cultural Logic of Late Capitalism* (Durham: Duke University Press, 1995), 282.

9. Historian David Lowenthal, one of the biggest critics of the idea and production of nostalgia, has called nostalgia a "deadly disease." He believes the propensity to create and consume nostalgia originated from the nineteenth century when many urban dwellers became homesick for the countryside back home. Today, nostalgia is still fed by urban anomie, technological change, and life in a world which harbors "the distempers of the contemporary rat race." See David Lowenthal, "Past Time, Present Place: Landscape and Memory," *The Geographical Review* LXV (January 1975): 1–36.

10. Pezzoni and Giles, 18.

11. Pezzoni and Giles, 18.

12. Pezzoni and Giles, 12. I have not been able to locate exactly what these "various histories" are, since all the accounts I have seen only describe Stover in a positive light.

13. Pezzoni and Giles, 13.

14. Darwin Lambert, *The Undying Past of Shenandoah National Park* (Boulder, CO: Roberts Rinehart, 1989), 22.

15. Lambert, 21.

16. These "forts," named for the cellars' roles as protective structures from American Indians, are discussed in Edward A. Chappell's "Acculturation in the Shenan-

doah Valley: Rhenish Houses of the Massanutten Settlement," in *Common Places: Readings in American Vernacular Architecture*, Dell Upton and John Michael Vlach, eds. (Athens, GA: University of Georgia Press, 1986), 27–57. Chappell doubts that the cellars were used for defensive purposes.

17. *Page: County of Plenty*, 14.

18. Andrea Sutcliffe, *Touring the Shenandoah Valley Backroads* (Winston-Salem, John F. Blair Publishers, 1999), 147.

19. Hugh Crandall and Reed Engle, *Shenandoah: The Story Behind the Scenery* (Las Vegas: KC Publications, 1990), 38.

20. "The Way of the Knights?" *Page News and Courier*, 29 March 2001.

21. "The Way of the Knights?"

22. Lambert, *The Undying Past of Shenandoah National Park*, 39.

23. Lambert, *Park*, 39.

24. *Page News & Courier,* 6 July 2000.

25. *Page News & Courier,* 6 July 2000.

26. Ballard, *Dismissing the Peculiar Institution: Assessing Slavery in Page and Rockingham Counties*, 4.

27. Ballard, *Dismissing*, 5.

28. Page County Heritage Association, *Interesting Page County Landmarks*, n.d., 2.

29. *Page: The County of Plenty*, 20; Pezzoni and Giles, *Page County Historic Resources Report*, 15.

30. Pezzoni and Giles, *Page County*, 18.

31. Gary Bauserman, "The History of Page County," in *Page: County of Plenty*, 21.

32. Russell H. Gurnee, *Discovery of Luray Caverns, Virginia* (Closter, NJ: R. H. Gurnee, 1978), 1.

33. "Confederate Monument, Luray, Virginia, Herbert Barbee, Sculptor," booklet of reprinted material from July 21, 1898 dedication, Page County Heritage Association, Luray, 1998.

34. Mary Baumgartner. Interview by the author. 4 February 1999.

35. Jocelyn Boswell. Letter to Author. September 1999.

36. Felicia Monroe. E-mail to the author. 9 July 2000.

37. Richard Maloney. E-mail to the author. February 2000.

38. Beatrice Baxter. Interview by the author. 13 May 2000.

39. Richard Sandler. Interview by the author. 22 June 1999.

40. G. Kurt Piehler, *Remembering War the American Way* (Washington, DC: Smithsonian Institution Press, 1995), 54.

41. Kirk Savage, *Standing Soldiers, Kneeling Slaves: Race, War, and Monument in Nineteenth-Century America* (Princeton: Princeton University Press, 1997), 170.

42. Savage, *Standing Soldiers*, 170.

43. Michael Kammen, *Mystic Chords of Memory*, 218.

44. *Page News and Courier,* 1 August 1913.

45. Savage, *Standing Soldiers*, 183.

46. Catherine W. Bishir, "Landmarks of Power: Building a Southern Past in Raleigh and Wilmington, North Carolina, 1885–1915," *Where These Memories Grow: History, Memory, and Southern Identity* (Chapel Hill: University of North Carolina Press, 2000), 139–68.

47. Kurt Piehler, *Remembering War the American Way* (Washington, DC: Smithsonian Institution Press, 1995), 62.

48. Savage, *Standing Soldiers*, 19.

49. *Confederate Monument, Luray, Virginia, Herbert Barbee Sculptor*, booklet published by Page County Heritage Association for rededication of Barbee Confederate Monument, based on excerpts from "Shenandoah Valley" New Market, VA by Ambrose L. Henkel, senior editor, n.d.

50. David Glassberg, *American Historical Pageantry: The Uses of Tradition in the Early Twentieth Century* (Chapel Hill: University of North Carolina Press, 1990), 23.

51. *Page: The County of Plenty*, 89.

52. *Page: The County of Plenty*, 41.

53. *Page: The County of Plenty*, 46.

54. Richard Goodwin. Interview by the author. 3 August 1999.

55. James Horton, "Presenting Slavery: The Perils of Telling America's Racial Story," *The Public Historian* (21, Fall 1999), 19–38.

56. Horton, "Presenting Slavery," 29.

57. Horton, "Presenting Slavery," 24.

58. "Shenandoah Dedicates New Stadium in Memory of War Dead," *Page News & Courier*, 6 July 1950.

59. "Depot Project Follows Tracks to Past," *Page News & Courier*, 5 October 2000, Special Supplement for the Page County Heritage Festival.

60. "Depot Project."

61. *Page News & Courier*. 30 December 1999.

62. "Page County Heritage Association Newsletter," February (1998), 1.

63. "Whatever Happened to the Luray Museum?" *Page County Heritage Association Newsletter*, June 2000, 3.

64. "Whatever Happened?"

65. Carl Butler. Interview by the author. 26 July 1999.

66. Dean MacCannell, "Reconstructed Ethnicity: Tourism and Cultural Identity in Third World Communities," *Annals of Tourism Research* (11, 1984), 375–91.

67. Gale Curtis. Interview by the author. 22 June 1999.

68. Michel Foucault, "Nietzsche, Genealogy, History," in *Language, Counter-Memory, Practice: Selected Essays and Interviews*, Donald F. Bouchard, ed. (Ithaca: Cornell University Press, 1977), 146.

69. "Ye Old Smiths," *Page News & Courier*, 3 March 1936.

Chapter Two

"... But Slavery Cured Us of That Weakness": The Search for the "Private" Public History of African Americans in Luray

African Americans hold a precarious position in the history of the Shenandoah Valley. As discussed in the previous chapter, the narratives *A Short History of Page County* by Harry Strickler and *A History of Rockingham County* by John Wayland are regarded as the official histories of this section of the Valley, and each author's deference to the German-Swiss pioneers, and their romanticization of a lost, agrarian lifestyle frame both the public and written histories of Luray and Page County. These mostly idyllic narratives (the exceptions being conflicts with Native Americans, as we have seen), leave out the documented fact that African Americans lived in the Valley, and the history of slavery receives only cursory mention. In fact, in both written and ethnographic sources, slavery is written off as not important to this area because it was not as extensive here as it was in other areas in Virginia. The response, "There just weren't many slaves here," was given on multiple occasions to my questions relating to the absence of African American history, and is reiterated in both Strickler's and Wayland's books.

This "low in number" assessment of enslaved people in Page County and the Shenandoah Valley serves to legitimize the near nonexistence of African Americans in historical narratives; the occasions in which they are mentioned are centered on discourses of slavery, not the fact that they had a significant influence on economic and social life in Luray. Over and over, my white informants and written sources indicated that African Americans were not here in great numbers. Although the numbers do seem low in comparison to the number of slaves in southeastern Virginia throughout history, this statistic is misleading. The whole notion of a "low number" theory is purely subjective and subject to interrogation: for example, a look at the census records of Page County in 1860 reveals that slave traders from more southern destinations came to this area, and purchased and resold many slaves, decreasing their numbers. Also, regardless of the seemingly low percentages, African Americans had a significant and lasting impact on the geography, economy, and cultural life of Page County: in 1885 a map of Luray indicates a region called "Darktown" where African Americans lived. Today, this section of Main Street remains predominantly African American. And, as we will see, historic properties important to the white community and white heritage are actually infused with stories of enslaved peoples and free blacks, but they are not part of the interpretive programs of the sites.

In this chapter I discuss two discrete, yet overlapping themes. First, the absence of African Americans in the historical narratives and public history of Luray is a result of a hegemonic, white commemorative landscape centered on historic homes of white forefathers, Confederate history, and the existence of white ancestral heritage groups, as discussed in chapter one. Luray, like many towns in the country, practices historical amnesia when it comes to African American history. Since the late nineteenth century, as regional southern memory began to perpetuate a Lost Cause mentality, African Americans were denied a place in collective southern memory and commemorative landscapes. Primary and ethnographic research suggests that although their contributions are left out of public and narrative history, African Americans were and are a vital part of the social and cultural life in Luray and the Shenandoah Valley. For example, a remarkable slave narrative written by Bethany Veney of Luray helps to shatter the myth of slavery as a one-dimensional system consisting of enslaved people laboring in the fields and kind masters overseeing their every move. New research is unearthing a history largely gone unnoticed, drawing attention to the African American presence in the Shenandoah Valley, and offering a fresh and perhaps radical perspective on popular conceptions of slavery.

Second, African American history in Luray revolves around a discourse of slavery—enslaved people are criminals rightfully hanged for killing their masters, or threatening owners and white women. At the same time, the purported unswaying benevolence of the white slave owners is incorporated into the public history of some of the more prominent historic sites in Luray as well as the narratives of some of my white informants. This ideology reinforces negative and false stereotypes of enslaved people (and white owners), but also ignores the actual social and cultural history of African Americans here. In this chapter, I will explore some of this neglected history and demonstrate how even the language in some primary historical documents reveals significant differences in how white and African American stories are told and transmitted through history.

A common image of slavery, reinforced by popular culture and historical accounts, consists of a large number of slaves working in the fields of sprawling plantations overseen by white masters on horses. This pervasive image does not accurately reflect the setting for all slaves, and certainly not for the slave society in the Shenandoah Valley. Instead, slaves worked in many capacities, from traveling with the first expedition across the Blue Ridge in 1670, to laboring on grain-producing farms. Both the physical and cultural landscapes here embody the presence of African Americans regardless of the population numbers.

Historian and local resident Dr. Charles Ballard has written about slavery and the contributions of African Americans in Page County. In his works, he explores African-American history by calling into question both Strickler's and Wayland's motives for excluding African Americans from their historical accounts. Ballard writes:

> The two authors were, perhaps, naturally reluctant to portray the early European settlers in a less than favorable light as sometime slaveholders. Moreover, such an image was intellectually contradictory and morally undermining to the more virtuous portrayal of Jefferson's ideal yeoman farmer society. Wayland and Strickler wrote uncritically of the sacrifices, hardships, and achievements of the first settler families.[1]

Strickler's account even goes as far as to suggest that slavery had been "thrust upon them [the Germans] largely by the force of circumstances," and that they "endured it willingly."[2] He further romanticizes Germanic Shenandoah Valley culture and its propensity to not have slaves by arguing that the inhabitants were not large slaveholders because they knew, firsthand, what it was to be subjugated:

> There must have been something in the Teutonic temperament, deep-seated and ineradicable, that revolted at the sight or thought of human chattels. It may be that the persecution and oppression that drove many of them out of Europe had left a smoldering fire within them that blazed up anew in the presence of chains.[3]

Although neither Strickler nor Wayland mention it, when the first pioneers entered this region in the early 1700s, African Americans were a part of this original group. In 1727, fifteen escaped Africans headed for the Blue Ridge Mountains, equipped with a desire for freedom and an arsenal of guns, and settled in Lexington, Virginia (approximately 75 miles south of Luray). After clearing land, raising crops, and erecting crude shelters, they were eventually caught, alarming colonial Governor Gooch who was worried that this settlement might serve as an example other escaped Africans might follow.[4]

Stories of slave rebellion in the early years of Blue Ridge settlement do
not have a place in Wayland's and Strickler's idyllic agrarian narratives as
they seek to preserve the constructed cultural identity of the pioneers as god-
fearing and anti-slavery. The omission of slavery is not surprising: Both Wayland and Strickler were descendents of pioneer families in the Valley, so any
discussion of enslaved African Americans would have tainted the image of
their own ancestors. Even today, descendents of the "first families" I inter-
viewed denied having slave owners in their families and also underplayed the
institution in the county, a subject discussed later in this work.

Strickler gives slavery and African Americans only cursory attention in his
book, but he does make an important acknowledgment regarding slavery in
the chapter devoted to the Civil War. His words still resonate in debates over
slavery's role in the Civil War:

> Some say that slavery was the cause of the war, others that State's rights was the
> cause. Both are partly right and partly wrong. Both of these questions were in-
> volved and you cannot discuss that conflict without considering both those is-
> sues. The country had the "States" rights fever but what caused the fever? Slav-
> ery was the bad tooth that caused the fever. The tooth was removed and the fever
> abated.[5]

Of course, the memory of slavery remains a "bad tooth" in the history of this
country, and issues are anything but gone. But it is telling that Strickler ad-
mits that the whole Civil War question cannot be considered without looking
at slavery. Most of my white informants, even though they deferred to Strickler's history, insisted that the war was about states' rights, not slavery. One informant said that slavery was "an unfortunate circumstance" of the war, and
another replied that the war could not have been about slavery since her ancestors who fought in the War did not own slaves.[6] Importantly, written de-
scriptions of notable historical properties appearing in newspaper articles and
archival documents suggest that the white owners (often the writers are direct
descendents) were always kind to their slaves. But the creation of a cultural
image of a benevolent slave owner not only blurs an accurate picture of slavery, it undermines the inclusion of African Americans in history: why would
slavery need to be discussed and maligned if nothing were wrong with it?

In Page County historical narratives, including Strickler's and Wayland's
works, and according to some county residents, Reconstruction went smoothly
because the area "never did depend entirely on slave labor."[7] The migration of
many African Americans out of the county during Reconstruction later helped
to give more credence to this belief. The two historians attribute the relative
ease of a return to economic and social normalcy to this "fact." However, a
more recent county history written in celebration of Page's bicentennial

claimed that Reconstruction was not as devastating in the county compared to other areas in the south because of Page's diverse economy—citizens were able to utilize natural resources to combat the destruction. Thus, the recovery of this area "was much faster in the Valley than in other parts of Virginia."[8] Although Africans Americans comprised a smaller percentage of the population in the Valley than in other parts of the country, and migrated to northern cities after the Civil War and into the twentieth century, they still were a vital force in both antebellum and post-bellum Page County. The alternative explanation to a quick and easy recovery after the Civil War offered by a local historian confirms that Wayland's and Strickler's theories can be disproved.

There is some evidence as well that the low number of slaves was due, in part, to large numbers of slaves being sold to southern slave dealers in the late 1850s. An article in the *PN&C* from 1942 reveals that "In 1856 [when] the southern slave buyers would come into this county and would buy slaves and take them to the south in large droves of colored men and women."[9] This evidence is based on one account by a local man, so it is difficult for it to be substantiated. Yet census records reveal that after 1860, the African American population declined.[10]

Perhaps what is most noteworthy in terms of the history of slavery in his recollection is the mention of a specific house and how "in front of the door of the house where 'Skeet' Good lives at Marksville was the place where they sold slaves."[11] A formerly enslaved woman who was born in nearby Augusta County in 1835 recalls being sold on a "sellin'" block.[12] Evidence also suggests that in Marksville, just a couple of miles north of Luray, slaves, including children, were sold on stepping stones or blocks in the entryways of homes. It was reported in a personal recollection in the *Page News & Courier* that:

> Mary Williams, then the mother of two little girls belonging to Paschal Graves, was with her little girl baby put on the block and sold to a man who took them away down south, then the other little girl was sold to Daniel Koontz for $400 and Mr. Koontz gave the little girl to Mrs. John P. Foltz, who lives at Newport, Mrs. Foltz being his daughter.[13]

If large slave auctions were not a part of slave culture in the Valley, placing slaves on blocks was still necessary, as slave dealers still needed to examine the property in which they were investing. Thus, historical evidence reveals an overlooked reality of slavery: that slaves were not just sold in public venues, but in more intimate, private settings. Whether or not this type of selling took place in other areas of the Valley and the country is a subject that is beyond the scope of this paper, but deserves academic attention. These types of transactions break the mold of popular conceptions of slave auctions set in town squares with many strangers looking on.

Slavery was a daily part of life in the Shenandoah Valley throughout the eighteenth and nineteenth centuries. Although it is given cursory mention in historical texts of the past and present, physical vestiges remain to begin to fill in the gaps in this region's history. In nearby Rappahannock County (30 miles east of Page), the Ben Venue plantation, built in 1844, includes three extant slave cabins that may be "the most architecturally sophisticated grouping of slave quarters surviving in Virginia."[14] These remarkable structures, listed on the state's register and the National Register, are visible markers on the landscape that slavery existed in the Valley. Not all markers are so visible, however. Noted in a local history book, *Madison County Homes,* are two houses containing slave whipping posts in their basements.[15]

Madison County (adjacent county southeast of Page, just over the Blue Ridge mountains) plays an important part in the history of African Americans in Luray and in Page County. Two African American informants described to me how African Americans came over the mountains from Madison County to settle in Page County in the early 1800s.[16] In Augusta County, the first free black settlement was established in the mid-eighteenth century, just after the first pioneers arrived here.[17] Today, the area just over the mountains into Page, Blainesville (formerly called Needmore), is the site of an African American community. The migration and settlement over the Blue Ridge into the outskirts of Luray at this time seems historically sound for two reasons. First, the mountains would have provided an excellent cover for escaping slaves from Madison County, or, perhaps, farther east, providing them the chance to begin new lives. Second, the opportunities for work at the Shenandoah Iron Works (SIW), founded in the county in 1836, may have provided the impetus for African Americans to settle here.

African American employees of the SIW, both free and enslaved, made a significant impact on the economic and social life in Page County before and after the Civil War. In February 1836, the SIW began operations at the southern edge of Page County, employing blacks and whites, slaves and freemen, and became "one of the foremost iron making enterprises in antebellum Virginia." Company housing created a multiracial village, including "rented" slaves from the Piedmont and Tidewater areas of Virginia. African Americans labored in the mines, the furnaces, and the fields; they were also employed as "forgemen, colliers, woodchoppers, clerks, teamsters. . . . There were others employed as wheelwrights, cartwrights, blacksmiths, farm laborers, and domestic servants."[18] That African Americans sought employment or found themselves employed in the iron industry in Page County should not be surprising; proficiency in ironworking can be traced to African roots. As John Vlach asserts, "The smelting of iron and the forging of wrought iron implements and sculpture are widely known throughout Africa."[19] Perhaps already equipped with ironmaking skills, a significant number of African Americans settled in antebellum Page County, literally and figuratively forging potentially better lives. The only free black property owner in Augusta County, Ned Tarr, was a respected blacksmith, running his own shop.[20] Further, slave labor was sought after since "white laborers were held to be less 'reliable' than slaves given the independent, material existence of many local whites."[21]

The Isabella Furnace, a neglected and overgrown site, and not noted in historical or tourist literature, tells a vital story of the African American community in Luray. Located just one mile north of Main Street on Route 340, Isabella Furnace was constructed in 1785, and depended on slave and free black labor. By 1841, Nicholas Yager bought the furnace and the surrounding plantation, and constructed quarters for his house servants. Today, the site of the furnace is a slightly hilly open field with two extant, yet decrepit stone buildings dotting the landscape.

When Yager purchased this large operation, including 3,189 acres of land, he also bought "33 Negroes with ten children," a rather large number of slaves for one plantation, and certainly not fitting the description of families in the Valley only owning just "a few" slaves.[22] The 1850 federal census indicates that Yager already owned fourteen slaves, and lists his occupation as "Miller." Combined then with the slaves he purchased with the Isabella site, he owned fifty-seven African Americans. His original fourteen slaves probably lived with Yager on Main and Court Streets in downtown Luray. Yager's home and shop in 1835 had more than 20 rooms, and local historian Terry Nale—based on her oral interviews with town residents—told me that slaves may have lived in the basement.[23] Nale, who also told me about the Yager home, has tried to gain access to the basement, but has been unable to do so. It is in front of this home where the purported slave auction block, the subject of chapter three, stood for many years until it was moved when the street was widened.

An esoteric document on Isabella Furnace handed to me by Nale, which she found in local history files in the public library, describes Yager's slaves as "helpers," and says "they were cared for both in body and spirit." H.W. Yager, a son of Nicholas, "had a chapel built and often were the times he read to them from a beautiful brown leather prayer book."[24] Written by Mrs. Henry McKay, a granddaughter of Nicholas Yager, this mysterious sheet provides an example of not only how difficult it is to find historical data on African Americans in Luray, but reinforces the ideology that white owners were caring and benevolent. And of course, Mrs. McKay, as a descendent of Yager, considered a prominent German settler in this area is unlikely to portray her ancestor as cruel to his slaves; such a description may taint *her* standing in the community.

Nearly one-third of the African American population in Page County in 1850 was free, and many were ex-slaves who had "either acquired their own

freedom through money raised from having been hired out during their lifetime, or had been freed by the wills of their very owners."[25] The African
Americans who worked for Yager probably fit in this category and helped lay
the foundation for the African American settlement on the west end of Main
Street, where many African Americans still live today. In the late nineteenth
century, with the assistance of organizations devoted to assisting freed slaves,
African American churches and schools were erected with this growth continuing into the twentieth century. After the Civil War, Yager sold part of his
plantation known as "Negro Hill," a name indicating the presence of African
Americans. By 1885, however, the name of this settlement changed to one
with racist overtones, "Darktown." Today it is still referred to as "The Hill,"
and, sometimes derogatorily as, "Nigger Hill."

Living and working in Page County helped free African Americans establish roots and contribute to the social and economic life of Luray, alongside
the white community. Because whites and African Americans lived and
worked together, interracial relationships were not uncommon, even though
they were illegal. In 1860, written evidence reveals that a white man, Haley
Morris, resided with a "mulatto" woman and five "mullato" children at the
SIW.[26]

Despite the existence of free blacks and the "low" number of African
Americans in Luray, slavery was a part of everyday life for nearly fifteen percent of Page County's population in 1850. The brutality of the institution was
no different here than from any other part of the state. We know this because
a first-hand account of an enslaved woman of Page County, Bethany Veney,
survives.

Born into slavery in 1815, Veney spent her slave years in Luray until two
visiting abolitionists bought her in 1858. She later settled in Worcester, Mass-
achusetts, where she composed her memoirs. Like most slave narratives,
Veney's story includes accounts of physical, sexual, and mental abuse, and
the tragic consequences of broken-up families. Veney's master, David Kibbler, was a "hard, ugly man," who enforced his authority by whippings. The
degradation she experienced is illuminated in passages like this one:

> Master Kibbler was a Dutchman,—a man of most violent temper, ready to fight
> anything or anybody who resisted his authority or in any way crossed his path.
> His one redeeming quality was his love for his horses and dogs. These must be
> fed before his servants, and their comfort and health always considered. He was
> a blacksmith by trade, and would have me hold his irons while he worked them.
> I was awkward one day, and he struck me with a nail-rod, making me so lame
> my mistress noticed it, and asked Matilda [Veney's sister] what was the matter
> with me; and when she was told, she was greatly troubled, and as I suppose
> spoke to Kibbler about it, for he called me to him, and bade me go a long way

off into a field, and, as he said, *cut some sprouts there*. But he very soon followed me, and cutting a rod, beat me severely, and then told me to 'go again and tell my mistress that he had hit me with a nail-rod if I wanted to.'[27]

This quote illustrates Kibbler's perverse preference to his animals before his slaves and the humiliating practice of having a slave find her own stick with which she would be beaten—power exercises very familiar to the culture of slavery. But Veney, like many other slaves, devised and employed complex mental methods of subverting her owner's dominance. In one episode, Veney accidentally caused Kibbler's horses to become erratic and they destroyed a side post of his fence. Irate, Kibbler told Veney to go find a hickory stick, presumably for whipping her. Instead of retrieving this object of abuse, she hid in the woods and decided to visit her master's father. Here, she knew she could get food, and, as it turns out, respite, because for a reason she could not figure out, the elder Kibbler would not beat her, even though he beat his own slaves. The elder Kibbler accompanied her back to her master's house and demanded she not be whipped. Her master obliged, and the threat of punishment was gone.

This account, and others like it in her narrative, are remarkable in demonstrating how complex, nuanced, and inconsistent the "peculiar institution" really was, even in the Shenandoah Valley. It seems odd, as it does to Veney, that the elder Kibbler would show sympathy for Veney. But perhaps what is at the heart of her being saved this one time was the relationship between father and son Kibbler. Was there a patriarchal battle taking place? Was there animosity between father and son? Was the elder Kibbler a more humane individual? Whatever the reason, Veney was used as a tool for the potential battle between father and son, showing again a slave's subhuman status. Veney, however, was not a passive agent in this familial relationship. She obviously knew how to circumvent a whipping, and must have known something about the relationship between the two Kibblers. Or, perhaps the slaves at both Kibbler homes shared information on the relationship of the two masters. Creating clandestine networks of information and exchanging news in a secretive fashion were common practices in a slave system. Veney, like many slaves, actively subverted the dominance of their masters, and her narrative provocatively reveals that even in an area with a "low" number of slaves, subverting the power structure of slavery was necessary for physical and mental survival. As Ira Berlin suggests in his seminal work on slavery, *Many Thousands Gone: The First Two Centuries of Slavery in North America*:

> For while slaveowners held most of the good cards in this meanest of contests, slaves held cards of their own. And even when their cards were reduced to near worthlessness, slaves still held that last card, which, as their owners well understood, they might play at any time.[28]

Veney's account also details another seldom explored complexity of the power dynamics within the slave system as she recalls being allowed to take work from outside her master's home. After being sold to a new master, David McKay, she was encouraged to find work "washing, cooking and field-work at planting and harvesting time." This way, when she was not needed on his property, McKay could still benefit from the slave's labor. But this certain degree of freedom also yielded power into the hands of Veney: she realized her earning potential and was able to negotiate with McKay: "After a while Mckay agreed that, if I should bring him one dollar and a half every Saturday night, he would be satisfied, and I could do what I pleased with myself."[29] During this time, Veney met and married her second husband, Frank (her first husband was sold, possibly to a more southern destination), and they resided in the mountains above Luray in a copper mine camp, where she cooked and cleaned for the workers. Veney's "freedom" to live away from her master, but, of course, to pay him, demonstrates an image of slavery different from the image of plantation and tyrannical, ever-present overseer. Although she was en-slaved, she lived apart from her master, and was able, to a surprising extent, to carve out a life for herself and her family. She and her husband were also lucky enough to have been purchased by two northern businessmen in 1858, and she moved to Rhode Island as a free woman.[30]

What was Veney's motivation for writing this account? Her story com-prises an introduction, preface, and two postscript letters written by a bishop and two ministers, and she discusses her strong Methodist faith, so perhaps her story is a religious tract extolling the virtues of the Methodist Church. Or, perhaps she was persuaded to record her life history because of a late nine-teenth century burgeoning of local and national African American historical societies. One such organization, the Boston Society for the Collection of Ne-gro Folklore, was founded at the same time her memoirs were published.[31] This movement was largely preservation-centered: African Americans, in-cluding W.E.B. DuBois, sought to capture and record African American folk culture, including "tales of southern black vernacular culture."[32] Or, her memoir might be an antisouthern, antislavery diatribe, a product of post-Civil War antagonism that continues today. And, of course, Veney could have sim-ply wanted to tell a painful story that she felt needed to be told.

Today Veney's narrative has become heritage. In 1998, her story was re-published by the Page County Heritage Association as a monograph. The re-publication of her memoir in a largely white, Confederate-heritage centered town was risky. A prominent member of Luray and historian commented:

The Heritage Association took a big step there by publishing those [mono-graphs] and there maybe was a fear of offending somebody, but Bob M [who is in charge of selling and overseeing publication of books] thinks it's great. I've got a couple dozen calls from people here in Page County whose ancestors owned slaves here in Page County and they don't mind opening the door. Maybe a generation or two further back in time would've been a different story but people are fascinated. It's almost like actually a badge, like well, we went through this. We were slave owners and that's part of our history and heritage. I always heard stories about my great-grandfather Kibbler and he was a mean son-of-a-bitch. He wouldn't just whip his niggers, he'd also whip everybody else too. White, everybody! And this was the main character in Bethany Veney's story, and I met his great-granddaughter who lives in Pass Run where Bethany lived and they're very open about it and I'm very pleased about it.[33]

Prompted by the publication of this work, local white citizens who have slaveowning ancestors are now wearing slave pasts like "badges" of pride — not pride in the slave system itself, but of having lived through it. Veney's slave story has become, then, a part of African-American heritage, but also of white heritage. Her narrative should elicit a shared heritage since whites and African Americans were intertwined in the slave system.[34]

Whatever the reasons behind its publication, Veney's account is an invaluable and remarkable resource for studying African-American history in Page County and in the country. It recounts the inhumanity of slavery in a geographical area believed to be unaffected by the institution, demythologizing historical texts and popular history accounts. The whipping posts found in the basements of homes, not in a public arena, suggest a decidedly different and more intimate picture of slavery here; Veney's narrative embellishes (and complicates) images of slavery as more than just a plantation system. We see from Veney's story how she learned to subvert the power structure she knew existed with slavery; we learn how she was allowed some "freedom" to travel and work away from the dominant eye of her master, and read how she used this freedom to create a better life. As a piece of local history, it contains names and places that can provide impetus for further research into African-American history and culture in the Valley. Perhaps most importantly, it serves as more proof that slaves and free blacks also contributed to the cultural and physical landscape of Page County in its early years; in fact, the pioneers, who are so revered in local history texts, would not have been able to attain their prominent status in the community and in history books were it not for African Americans.

The other noted history of an African American in Luray is the story of Mann Page, a slave who bought his, his wife's, and his son's freedom in 1831. According to Strickler, Page was a blacksmith who was most likely named after the white Mann Page of Gloucester County, Virginia.[35] In fact, Page County was named for a descendent of the white Mann Page. Strickler somewhat sarcastically claims that maybe the county "was named for Mann Page, the blacksmith!"[36] At any rate, Mann Page, ex-slave, was also able to write, as he signed his will in this same year. Page, like Veney, broke the bonds of slavery to attain status as a free person of color. But unlike Veney, we have no record of Page's experience.

The western or African American section of the town of Luray is dotted with churches, a visible reminder of the influence of African American culture here. African American churches in Luray, many of which are still standing, are visible proof that the African American community wanted to take part in and alter the cultural landscape of Luray. Moreover, many of the African American churches, standing directly on Main Street and not hidden on overgrown hilltops are evidence that African Americans wanted to worship, but also to carve out visible proof that they too belonged on Main Street.

The church was and is a vital part of African-American culture, and Luray boasts a strong church presence. As Elizabeth Clark Lewis writes:

The church was a pivotal part of the African American community's efforts to protect family and social life from white intervention. . . . God not only promised to deliver all African Americans as an oppressed people but also provided a palliative philosophy to counteract the social and occupational dehumanization they experienced daily. At the same time, the worship service addressed their profound need for economic and social redemption in the present world.[37]

Surely Bethany Veney's account shows that African Americans in Luray faced the type of "dehumanizing" treatment that Clark Lewis describes, and constructed churches to serve as sanctuaries and as venues for community building. Before the Civil War there were no designated churches for African Americans: whites and blacks worshipped together. With freedom and the assistance of white missionaries, today there are four African American churches. Two, Bethel Baptist and St. John's Baptist are on Luray's Main Street. Another St. John's Baptist lies in Salem (just west of Luray), and Mt. Carmel Baptist stands in Blainesville, where whites and blacks worshipped together as late as 1898.

St. John's Baptist in Luray was a log cabin schoolhouse designed to assist in educating newly freed slaves. The renovated church is now 128 years old, and services are still held here. Across the street from Luray's Singing Tower, a carillon of 47 bells, sits Bethel Baptist, first established in 1888. The Reverend W.W. Davenport, who began preaching in the home of a local citizen, built the church, but it was destroyed by a storm.[38] It was rebuilt, and with the assistance of a white pastor from Baltimore, the church was finally completed.

The transition from worshipping privately in a log schoolhouse, in a congregation member's home, or in white churches where African Americans often had to sit in separate sections to constructing churches directly on Main Street reveals how emancipation and African Americans' desires to be vital members of the community transformed Luray's landscape. Unfortunately, a more complete picture of African American history here is extremely difficult to piece together. As a prominent Valley historian relayed to me:

> As far as what's available for African Americans in Page history (prior to 1860) the best thing to do is tap into the census records. Slave schedules and free black as well as will inventories. Otherwise (and this applies to nearly the entire Valley) it's a real head-beating situation."[39]

And although not much history has been recorded, African American history in Luray can also be explored through the lens of white vestiges on the landscape, many of which are noted historic sites. These sites, largely devoted to the founding families and to the Civil War era, do not mention a shared heritage. But further exploration of them reveals a shared history, and a history centered on African American slaves, not on African Americans as influential settlers of the town.

Most of these structures, as outlined in chapter one, reflect a white, eighteenth century history, and are devoted to preserving an idealized, romanticized image of Luray's pioneer families. Published in 1962, *Old Homes of Page County* describes homes of historically prominent white citizens and is an important book for residents and historians.[40] In the most recent Historic Resources Survey Report completed in 1998, these structures are reaffirmed as historical standouts, and as embodying Page's heritage. Certainly many of these sites, as we have seen, are extremely important artifacts well worthy of preservation and interpretation, and of vital importance to Shenandoah Valley history. The *PN&C* often highlights specific celebrations, anniversaries, and events occurring around these sites because of their strong connection to local history and local citizens. But these structures serve another purpose—they are reminders of exclusion and white supremacy and legitimate the current power structure.[41] More succinctly, the roles of historic structures—as tourism sites and as markers of a dominant white community identity—is not such a simple duality. Although the sites appear to be symbols of a unified vision of the past, they are not.

Once such site is the Ruffner House, a federal-style, mid-nineteenth century historic house built by descendents of early pioneers to the Valley, Peter and Mary Ruffner, who first laid claim to the land. Currently a bed and breakfast, the home is important as an artifact belonging to a founding white family, and as a remnant of ancestry, as there are a number of Page County residents who are descendents of the Ruffners.

Three years ago, a Ruffner family reunion took place, drawing family members from all over the country, and the event was covered by the *PN&C*.

Events that took place over the reunion weekend included a tour of other historic sites in Page Valley, picnics, and a dedication of a monument to Peter and Mary Ruffner. There was also a living history presentation focused on the relationship between Booker T. Washington, and William Henry Ruffner, Washington's last owner. Ruffner illegally educated Washington and "paid for his college education if he would build a school in Charleston, South Carolina."[42] Washington kept his promise.

Other Ruffners were slave owners, including Rueben of Page County, Virginia. According to his obituary ". . . he was a large slave owner for this section and though at all times he required exemplary industry of his dependents, he was known as a just and generous master. . . . He was honored by the love and devotion of his colored people throughout his life. . . ."[43] This description is used not to vilify Ruffner for being a slave owner, but to point out how African American history is told through a lens of slavery and of a benevolent slave owner. What the article also yields, however, is more evidence of African Americans in Page County and the culture they created together.

The apparent shared history between the Ruffners and African Americans does not translate into a shared heritage. The descendents of the Ruffners may know about the presence of African Americans, especially the provocative and important story of William Henry Ruffner and Booker T. Washington, but most of Luray's other citizens, and especially the visitors to the bed and breakfast, do not. And, dedicating a monument to the original pioneers continues to reinforce a single view of heritage—that those most deserving of a memorial in the community were white. Thus, the founding families maintain a heritage monopoly over the town, and through public history hold a framework designed to show that history in Luray "naturally" evolved through white families and lineages only.[44]

White hegemony in public history sites is ubiquitous in the United States, but in the South, because of the presence of slavery in its history, the absence of African American history has a long-standing precedent. When the white Democratic elites used the Confederate past as a political tool to gain power in the 1890s, African Americans were relegated to a subservient role in the creation of public heritage. As W. Fitzhugh Brundage argues:

> For a century after the Civil War public representations of southern history conspicuously ignored any recognition of the recalled past of blacks. African Americans created their own understanding of their past, but whereas white social memory was both public and universal in its claims, the black countermemory was neither. Through the activities of African American fraternal lodges, churches, schools, and civic groups, blacks certainly imagined their history. But these expressions were either ignored by or were largely invisible to whites.[45]

In Luray, as in many areas of the South, public history still has yet to fully incorporate African American history. As I demonstrated above, African Americans built churches and schools to create a culture far removed from slavery and oppression, but these efforts are not acknowledged by whites and are not incorporated in the primary narratives, the landscape, and tourist literature.

My exploration of the Ruffner family and the reunion event is not to denigrate personal notions of family pride and heritage; it is simply to interrogate the ways in which heritage excludes the lives and livelihoods of African Americans who made heritage events like the Ruffner reunion possible. The press coverage of the event *did* discuss the Ruffners as slave owners, so the subject is not neglected. But what is provocative here is that a *mixed* history may be admitted, but there seems to be no place for African Americans in a shared, public heritage of the Ruffner family. The new monument to Peter and Mary attests to this claim.

Mauck Meeting House, a structure overseen by the PCHA (and mentioned in chapter one), is also a site reflecting a shared history but not heritage. From 1809 to 1860, African slaves attended services at Mauck, segregated to seating in upstairs galleries.[46] This fact is absent from interpretation of the site.

The interpretation at Mauck and the inclusion of an African American historical presence could be beginning to change, however. The annual Christmas Sing held at Mauck, one of the most popular events the PCHA holds, has, for two consecutive years, hosted an African American gospel choir led by Frank Hall, my chief African American informant. The first year the event was held (1999) proved to be one of the most emotionally moving experiences of my life, and similarly affected other members as well. The concert was very well-attended, drawing only whites from the community, and of these, mostly members of the PCHA. The acts before Frank's choir, a hammered dulcimer player, and the high school barbershop quartet created an upbeat, jovial atmosphere. This all changed when the choir started singing. Realizing that his organ was not working, Frank borrowed an elderly man's cane and used it as a stomp stick to keep the rhythm. The sound of the voices, the profound meaning of songs like "Gonna Hide Behind That Mountain" and the sight of the setting winter sun and the Blue Ridge Mountains outside the windows elicited tears from many members of the audience. When the choir finished singing and the master of ceremonies needed to announce the next act, she had to step away from center stage, overcome with emotion.

In 2000, the choir had to perform an abbreviated service because of time constraints, but its return and probable invitation for years to come shows that African American heritage—here in the form of gospel music—has a place in the public history of Luray. I told Frank that I found out that African Americans worshipped here in the early 1800s, and he, perhaps, will make that announcement at the next Sing, making the white audience aware of a shared history and shared heritage of this site.

If cursory mention is made of African American history in some of the historically prominent sites in Luray, there is a historical area where African American history is nonexistent: the Civil War. Civil War memory, as we have seen, dominates the physical and cultural landscape of Luray, especially in the form of historical highway markers, the two Confederate soldier monuments, and local public events. The newest community organization devoted to the Civil War is the Page County Civil War Commission (PCCWC) formed in 1999. The mission of the commission is to "actively encourage, support, and participate in preservation projects and the documentation of papers and artifacts connected with places, people, or events that specifically relate to Page County's unique role in the American Civil War."[47] Membership includes local citizens, historians, members of the United Daughters of the Confederacy, and the Sons of the Confederate Veterans. Of significant importance to the group is the erection of signs at sites important to Page County's involvement in the Civil War, erected through the Civil War Trails markers statewide program. This initiative and the Civil War as tourist attraction will be further discussed in chapter four.

One of the newest roadside markers sponsored by the Virginia Department of Transportation and based on the initiative of the current president of the PCCWC is a sign dedicated to two Page County Confederate soldiers who were executed in 1865 *after* the surrender at Appomattox. Sentenced to death for stealing horses, which they actually returned, Summers and Koontz were memorialized in June 1999, 134 years after they died. The commemoration received significant local press coverage in the *PN&C* and drew costumed actors and confederate reenactors. One article described the dedication as an important event "because it was a tragedy that never should have happened in the first place."[48] Although not many people attended the event, the marker stands on Route 340 in front of Page County High School.

By contrast, a couple of miles south of the center of town lies the unknown spot of the execution of two other Page County residents, the slaves Cap and Mart, who were hanged in 1842 for murdering their master, John Wesley Bell. According to historical accounts, Cap and Mart were sent to their deaths eating ginger cakes and beer they received in exchange for their bodies which were to be used for the "furtherance of the medical profession."[49] After their deaths, the Bell estate was given $914.28, the "value" of the two men.[50]

Both sets of executions and the narratives which describe them illustrate not only how different white and black history is treated in historical accounts, but also how African American history in Luray is told through slave rebellions and murder—a sensationalist perspective. Also, the various texts that describe the story of the two men, an 1898 newspaper article, a 1911 account, a 1950 account and a 1997 account, have contributed to the creation of the factual occurrence as myth, and they are replete with inaccuracies. For example, the 1911 account claims the date of the executions as 1842. In the 1950 article, the year became 1843. The most recent account lists 1842 as the date of the executions. Another inconsistency stems from the exact spot of the hangings. The 1997 article claims it is located outside of town, where the 1950 account claims it could have been in town, just off Main Street at the site of the current Mimslyn Inn.[51]

Inconsistencies are, of course, to be expected in historical accounts, but there seem to be no debates in the story of Summers and Koontz as there are with Cap and Mart. In fact, in my experience speaking with citizens and historians about the Civil War and listening to various talks on battles and historical figures, specific dates and places were often named. Being precise about who did what and where is a vital part of Civil War memory—white Civil War memory. Tracing one's lineage in order to qualify for membership to the UDC or SCV is a precise, exclusionary exercise. Reenactors painstakingly research even buttons on uniforms, sometimes soaking them in urine to achieve patina.[52] This phenomenon does not, however, carry over into African American history. Could this specificity be, then, hegemonic? Giving attention to family lineages and exact battles and dates protects Civil War memory from being understood in any other way than these "facts." The story of the actual crimes and the subsequent executions differ, too. Nowhere in the dedication to Summers and Koontz is any graphic detail included about their tragic fate; this type of description would probably be viewed as an insult to their memory. For Cap and Mart, however, as with newspaper stories of other slaves in Page, gruesome facts are very much a part of the history of the events. In describing the murder of John Wesley Bell, even the most recent *PN&C* account includes gore:

> Having been out about 250 yards from the Bell home, the slaves were busy cutting bushes along a branch. Apparently, Bell came out to the job and while speaking to "Captain" was struck by a blow from behind by "Martin." The axblow easily busted Bell's skull and killed him instantly. At once setting to hide the evidence of the murder, "Captain" repositioned Bell's head into the stream so that the blood from the crime would be washed away. A larger problem was the cedar log which their master had falled against and spattered with blood. Chopping away the bark of the log, the slaves piled it on the ground and concealed it under the brush. The snowfall the same night aided in disguising the bloodied chips. . . .[53]

The execution of Cap and Mart also is described in grim language:

> . . . The prisoners were marched on foot from the jail with their hands tied be-
> hind them and ropes around their necks. . . . Martin and Captain were made to
> stand erect in the wagon while the sheriff and the deputy tied the ropes attached
> to their necks to the arm of the gallows and then the wagon was driven from be-
> neath leaving the bodies swinging in the air.[54]

The executions of Summers and Koontz, however, are couched in very different terms:

> . . . the two Page County men were executed shortly after entering the camp at
> Rude's Hill. When Summers's father arrived the next day, he found both men ly-
> ing on the ground, their heads propped up on rocks, as though they were sleep-
> ing. Letters they had written in their last moments alive, to their loved ones, were
> given to Mr. Summers and he took the bodies back to Page County for burial.[55]

The two soldiers are described as martyrs dying peacefully, with no mention
of the blood that must have been a part of the scene, since they were shot to
death. The soldiers' deaths are tragic, the slaves' deaths are presented in gory
detail. Although Cap and Mart can be considered martyrs, too, their story is
not even given the possibility for this interpretation: They simply died as
cold-blooded murderers.

For the most part single slave stories frame the legacy and cultural identity
of African Americans in Page County, and important sites on the landscape
associated with African American history, including the Isabella Furnace, are
left out of tourism literature and the *PN&C*. And although a few years ago the
PN&C explored the history of the African American congregations and mentions events associated with Black History Month, African American heritage
and culture remains separate from white heritage and culture. As I have
shown, the history and heritage of Luray are shared by both whites and
African Americans, but has not been a part of public history here until recently. In July 1998, a purported slave auction block became the most contested piece of public history in Luray, the subject of the following chapter.

Eric Gable and Richard Handler examined the "authority of documents"
and the production of history and historical interpretation in their ethnographic work at Colonial Williamsburg (CW). Through participant observation and interviews, they concluded that front-line interpreters are told not to
stray from documented fact, and not to engage in storytelling, which is considered unprofessional. Gable and Handler argue that adherence in public history to documents along with administrative documents created by the upper
echelons of the institution and handed to the front-line interpreters, answers

CW's need to be "authoritative, but not authoritarian,"[56] and that "documented facts, more than complex narratives, can be used for types of control and accountability that employees at all levels of the corporate hierarchy seem to accept."[57] I suggest that the requirement for history to be based in fact—in primary written documents—smacks of historical control which, ultimately, leads to a public history devoid of personal stories, and oral tradition, and ends up as simply a written description on a plaque. The net effect is not only a mundane form of historical commemoration, but an exclusionary history, insisting it must only rely on "facts" and defining "facts" as necessarily derived from written records. In "Nietzsche, Genealogy, History," Foucault also is concerned with claims of "truth" and "origins" in historical practice, and decries the construction of a linear, progressive history obsessed with objective and predetermined truths:

> The world we know is not this ultimately simple configuration where events are reduced to accentuate their essential traits, their final meaning, or their initial and final value. On the contrary, it is a profusion of entangled events. . . . We want historians to confirm our belief that the present rests upon profound intentions and immutable necessities. But the true historical sense confirms our existence among countless lost events, without a landmark or a point of reference.[58]

Equipped with an authority endowed upon them by the public, the historian who is preoccupied with absolutes and facts ignores the "lost events," the never-recorded and never-memorialized people and landscapes. According to Foucault, "lost events," nevertheless, constitute the essence of history, and are, unfortunately, tossed aside in efforts to construct a documented, one-dimensional, and limited version of history, grounded in issues of power.

In the next chapter, I consider the "lost" event of the dedication of Luray's "Ol Slave Auction Block" in July 1998. Although a nondescript structure on the landscape, embedded in it are myriad ideas and ideologies revolving around power, memory, history, race, and public history. I ultimately contend that this subversive artifact stands as a celebration of heritage, oft-criticized by contemporary scholars, and that these kinds of artifacts can help to enrich and diversify our historical and commemorative landscapes.

NOTES

1. Charles C. Ballard, *Dismissing the Peculiar Institution: Assessing Slavery in Page and Rockingham Counties, Virginia* (Luray, VA: 1998), 3.

2. Harry M. Strickler, *A Short History of Page County* (Harrisonburg, VA: 1974), 179–80.

3. Strickler, *A Short History*, 180.

4. J. Suzanne Simmons, "They Too Were Here: African-Americans in Augusta County and Staunton, Virginia, 1745–1865," Master's Thesis, James Madison University, May 1994.

5. Strickler, *A Short History*, 190.

6. Richard Sandler. Interview by the author. 22 June 1999; Jocelyn Boswell. Letter to the author. September 1999.

7. Strickler, *A Short History*, 197.

8. *Page: County of Plenty*, 21.

9. *Page News & Courier*, 29 January 1932.

10. "A forgotten people—Page County's antebellum population of African Americans," *Page News & Courier*, "Heritage and Heraldry" column, 17 June 1999.

11. "A forgotten people."

12. Suzanne Simmons, "They Too Were Here," 50.

13. *Page News & Courier*, 29 January 1932.

14. Calder Loth, ed. *Virginia Landmarks of Black History* (Charlottesville: 1995).

15. Vee Dove, *Madison County Homes* (Madison County, VA: 1975).

16. Karl Lilly. Interview by the author. July 1999.

17. J. Suzanne Simmons, "They too were here: African-Americans in Augusta County and Staunton, Virginia, 1745–1865," M.A. Thesis, Department of History, James Madison University, Harrisonburg, Virginia, 1994, 71.

18. Charles Ballard, *From Iron Plantation to Company Town: The Shenandoah Iron Works, 1836–1907* (Luray, VA: Page County Heritage Association, 1998), 10.

19. John Vlach, *The Afro-American Tradition in Decorative Arts* (Athens, GA: University of Georgia Press, 1990), 129.

20. Simmons, "They Too Were Here," 11.

21. Ballard, *From Iron Plantation to Company Town*, 11.

22. "Isabella Furnace and Settlement," information sheet given to author by Terry Nale, historian. Owned by author, (n/d).

23. Terry Nale. Interview by the author. 20 May 2000.

24. Nale interview.

25. Robert H. Moore II, "Family Profiles of Page's Antebellum African-American Population," *Page News & Courier,* 3 September 1999.

26. Moore, "Family Profiles," 1999.

27. Betheny Veney, *Aunt Betty's Story: The Narrative of Bethany Veney, A Slave Woman.* (Luray, VA: 1998), 11.

28. Ira Berlin, *Many Thousands Gone: The First Two Centuries of Slavery in North America* (Cambridge, MA: Harvard University Press, 1998), 2.

29. Veney, *Aunt Betty's Story,* 10.

30. Frank Veney did not accompany Bethany to the north, for reasons left unstated in her narrative. He remained in Luray and purchased property on "The Hill."

31. Jeffrey C. Stewart and Fath Davis Ruffins, "Afro-American Public History in Historical Perspective, 1828–1984 in *Presenting the Past: Essays on History and the Public*, Susan Porter Benson, Stephen Brier, Roy Rosenzweig, editors (Philadelphia: 1986).

32. Stewart and Ruffins, "Afro-American Public History," 312.

33. Carl Butler. Interview by the author. 26 July 1999.

34. According to some of my white informants and one of my African American informants, Veney's story has been positively received in the community.

35. Harry M. Strickler, *A Short History of Page County, Virginia* (Harrisonburg, VA, 1974), 138.

36. Strickler, *A Short History*, 138.

37. Elizabeth Clark-Lewis, *Living In, Living Out: African American Domestics and the Great Migration* (New York: 1994), 34.

38. "Black Congregations Contribute to Page's Rich Heritage," *Page News and Courier*, 1 September 1998.

39. Richard Maloney. E-mail to the author. 2 January 2000.

40. Jennie Ann Kerkhoff, *Old Homes of Page County* (Luray, VA: 1962).

41. Martha Norkunas, *The Politics of Public Memory: Tourism, History, and Ethnicity in Monterey, California* (Albany, SUNY Press, 1993), 8.

42. "Ruffner Clan to Meet for Big Reunion in Luray," *Page News and Courier*, 5 July 1997.

43. *Page News & Courier*, 25 June 1905.

44. Norkunas, *The Politics of Public Memory*, 93.

45. W. Fitzhugh Brundage, "No Deed But Memory," in *Where These Memories Grow: History, Memory, and Southern Identity*, W. Fitzhugh Brundage, editor (Chapel Hill: University of North Carolina Press, 2000), 1–28.

46. *Page: County of Plenty*, 110.

47. *The Sentinel*, Vol. 1, No. 1, July 1999, 1.

48. *Page News and Courier*, 1 July 1999.

49. *Page News and Courier*, 12 January 1950.

50. Robert H. Moore, II, "The Controversial 19th Century Murder of John Wesley Bell," *Page News and Courier*, 20 November 1997.

51. The hanging of Cap and Mart was a well-attended event. According to an article in the *Page News and Courier* for August 8, 1898, the event saw "people thick as blackbirds."

52. Tony Horwitz, *Confederates in the Attic* (New York: 1999).

53. *Page News & Courier*, 20 November 1997.

54. *Page News & Courier*, 18 July 1911.

55. "Yankees Executed Confederate Soldiers," *Page News & Courier*, 2 July 1998.

56. Eric Gable and Richard Handler, "The Authority of Documents at Some American History Museums," *Journal of American History* (June 1994), 133.

57. Gable and Handler, "The Authority," 135.

58. Michel Foucault, "Nietzsche, Genealogy, History," in *Language, Counter-Memory, Practice: Selected Essays and Interviews* (Ithaca: Cornell University Press, 1977), 155.

Chapter Three

Subverting Heritage and Memory: Luray's "Ol' Slave Auction Block"

On an overcast June day in 1999, I sat down with my first informant, Bill. Equipped with a tape recorder and a notepad of questions, I began to talk to this gentleman, the president of the local and prestigious heritage association about the history and heritage of the town. I was not surprised to hear Bill talk about the Confederate monuments, as Civil War history dominates the public history of Luray, the Shenandoah Valley, and many other areas of Virginia. I expected our interview to be a history lesson on Confederate troops in the Valley, and the popular "burning" of the Valley by Union General Phillip Sheridan in 1864, an event very significant in the town's history and collective memory.

But after my informant mentioned the two prominent monuments, his tone lowered, and he began to tell me about a certain controversy which arose the previous year (June 1998) when the PCHA, supported by the town government and many of its citizens, rededicated the Barbee monument. As I discussed in chapter one, the rededication one hundred years after the first dedication, was as grand an affair as it was in 1898, featuring reenactors, parades, and community singing.

Near the center of town, Bill said, another commemoration was taking place: a counterdedication to a purported slave auction block sponsored by a local African American citizen. His ceremony consisted of a few supporters, a wreath-laying, and a plaque-mounting bearing the inscription, "In memory of the Black men, women, and children who were put upon this 'Slave Auction Block' to be displayed and sold. May we remember, too, the social system that placed them there." The citizen's agit-prop action gained press coverage in the local paper and stood out in the minds of Bill and many other white informants even a year after the event. Not knowing anything about a slave block or Luray's African American community, I went to the local library, and looked up the commemoration in the paper. After realizing that this counter and more private event was significant to a study of public history, I knew that the scope of my research now included public history, cultural identity, tourism, and race.

In this chapter, I explore this extremely complex and important public history site that embodies, echoes, and reflects African American history and memory and the contemporary racial tensions that underlie it. First, I argue that resolutions focused on coming to terms with slavery, including dedicating the auction block, are made especially difficult as any criticism expressed against Confederate heritage is seen as an *attack,* relying on an ideology of "northern aggression" and victimization. This perspective not only sets African Americans who do not support Confederate heritage on the offensive, but also makes them become aggressors, reinforcing a stereotype of barbarism. In the face of this adversity, some white and African American citizens have sought to reclaim heritage, history, and equitable treatment by formally organizing into a citizen's group, Concerned Citizens for Equality (CCE), and by drawing attention to Luray's "Ol Slave Auction Block."

Second, because African American history and public history revolve around a strong oral tradition, they are often not readily revealed on the landscape and are, in the case of Luray, overlooked because they lack "factual" or written documentation. This refusal to recognize oral tradition as "real" history is not simply limited to Luray: consider the very guidelines for historic designation at the local, state, and national levels. Most of these standards require *documentation* of the site's historical importance, leaving out the possibility that its history and significance was not written down and exists in a more oral realm. I suggest that new methodologies and perspectives are needed for unearthing African American history, and that performing ethnographic work combined with cultural landscape study offers a promising solution. I also argue that African American commemorative activities and celebrations of heritage should be considered with an emphasis on churches and other more private venues and events that have been important to African American culture over time.

Third, I discovered that performing ethnographic work in a racially-charged environment yields new perspectives on the ethnographic process itself and subverts the traditional us/them relationship: how could I have been the only outsider in this situation when it was clear that African Americans are also outsiders to the practice of heritage here? Surreptitiously traveling back and forth between speaking with whites and African Americans, and having to keep hidden from each "side" what I discovered, put me in a precarious ethnographic location.

Part of what I kept "hidden" from my African American informants and battled with academically and emotionally was realizing that Confederate heritage is revealed very strongly in my white informants' private lives and in the public history in Luray. Who was I to tell these informants that they are wrong, misguided, and even racist as they honor their ancestors and town fathers? Ethnographic fieldwork, combined with a cultural landscape study, which frames this work, helped me realize the complexity of these issues, in ways simply studying the landscape and primary sources could not have yielded. I better understood how heritage is not simply about Black versus White: not all my White informants supported Confederate heritage and opposed the dedication of the block, and not all African Americans were upset by Confederate heritage. Ethnography helped me to desert binary oppositions and explore the nuances of heritage and race relations.

While I believe that public displays of Confederate heritage are vital to private and public identity in Luray, I also believe that Confederate memory is founded upon beliefs which purposefully exclude African Americans and their history. The auction block, the only publicly commemorated African American history site, has been criticized and defaced by a white citizen, determined not to allow a public commemoration to occur. While this individual could have been working alone and has made other white citizens angry, support for African American history on the landscape has not been taken up by the PHCA. Thus, white, hegemonic Confederate memory does not allow room on the commemorative landscape for African American expressions of heritage. This exclusion, however, does not signify that African American communities have never celebrated history or heritage; on the contrary, African Americans began commemorations devoted to the elimination of the slave trade as long ago as the early nineteenth century.[1]

Finally, by using the slave auction block as an example, I challenge some current academic theories that claim that the practice of heritage is false and misguided, and saturated in nostalgia. This block is proof that notions of heritage are paramount to personal and community identity, and that African American public history and material culture have the power to subvert the status quo by their very presence.

The slave auction block is sandstone, measures 17" x 20½" in section and is approximately 58" high (figure 8). It stands next to the Massanutten School building and behind the Luray Train Depot in the central location of Inn Lawn Park, an important heritage and touristic space in Luray. Dark stains on the stone, scraped in the fall of 1999 to determine if they were blood, are key markings and will be discussed later in this chapter.

The slave block, prior to dedication, remains an historical enigma. According to an historical account written in 1961, the stone lay at the corner of

Figure 8.   Slave Block

Court and Main Streets in downtown Luray for fifty years.[2] When Main
Street was widened in the same year, it was placed inside a nearby building.
The mayor of Luray at that time asked that the block be moved to Inn Lawn
Park, where he wanted it recognized with a brass plaque. This was never
done, however, possibly because the stone's authenticity could never be determined. The stone then sat unmarked next to the library where it has stood
for the last forty years. Frank, the African American citizen responsible for
dedicating the block, first found out about the stone's history as a slave block
from an African American citizen whom he was driving around town one day.
Shocked by her claim, he forged his journey to explore the block's history
culminating in the dedication in July 1998.

   One of the strangest elements in the story of the slave block is that it sat in
its current location *unmarked* for forty years. Some older residents with
whom I spoke remember the block and its near-dedication in 1961, but most
of my white informants who had been told about the legend simply disbe-
lieved it was an auction block and said it was a stepping block used to mount
horses.[3] Thus, counter arguments against the stone being a slave auction
block are also a part of this monument's history. In 1961, the *PN&C* wrote
that it was "a mount for horseback riders."[4] A white informant told me that it
was highly unlikely slaves in Luray were auctioned off since there were probably no full-fledged auctions in this area of Virginia, unlike Richmond or

Alexandria (see chapter two).[5] And, verification of the block's existence on Main Street is not mentioned in either *Page: County of Plenty*, or Strickler's *A Short History of Page County*, two of the principal historical narratives of the town. Certainly there is credence in the reasons the stone is not a slave auction block, but the exclusion of the stone in the two written narratives should be viewed with caution. As we have already seen, these works lack a comprehensive history of African Americans in Luray.

This block, either on its side or standing upright *could have been* a slave auction block. According to my informants who believe it is only a stepping stone, the fact that a stepping stone could very well have been an auction block is not considered. It is also important to note that the location of the block on Court and Main Streets (it is not known how long it stood there) was, at one time, the home of Nicholas Yager, a slave owner whose slaves lived in the basement of the building. As I argued in the previous chapter, contrary to popular conceptions of slave auctions being held in public spaces and only in geographical areas with large numbers of slaves, written evidence suggests that slave buying and selling did occur in more private settings—like the doorways of individual homes—in the Shenandoah Valley, and elsewhere in the United States.

In Spring 1999, I told Frank about a distinguished forensic anthropologist from George Washington University, Dr. James Starrs, who would probably have an interest in the block. Dr. Starrs agreed to come to Luray to test some dark stains on the block's surface without remuneration, and in September, Starrs brought a team of experts to Luray. The event received front-page coverage in the "Page County Plus" section of the *PN&C* with photographs of the team in action.[6]

It was not until early in 2000 that the forensic report was passed on to Frank. According to the results, the maroon stain "is most consistent with a possible blood splatter, noting the darker lichen growth in the sunken contours and cracks of the stone."[7] Intriguingly, the report also claims that the stain was "most likely spilled or dripped from about 4 feet above the top horizontal surface."[8] Even if it were proven that the stain was blood, it is not known whether or not the blood was white or African American. The investigative team could not, therefore, truly authenticate the stone as a slave auction block.

For all of the press the testing of the stains on the block received, the events of the previous two years—the counter dedication and the visit by the forensic experts—seemed to vanish from the pages of the *PN&C* and with my white informants. Instead, the newest preservation project, the renovation of the train depot (which is just across the railroad tracks from the block and is visible from the location of the block) has taken the historical spotlight. The Page

County Civil War Commission (PCCWC) discussed the possibility of acknowledging the stone as a *symbol* of an auction block in February 2000. As proposed by the PCCWC, it would be situated next to a new Civil War kiosk, devoted to telling the history of the Civil War in Page County. But the new president of the PCCWC has given no indication that he is interested in the slave block as part of Civil War history. In fact, at present he is more interested in pursuing the history of African Americans who fought for the Confederacy, arguing that those who fought "not necessarily under duress" is drastically higher than history books and popular culture would have the public believe.[9]

During my research and fieldwork, I also noticed articles about a new organization in the county, Concerned Citizens for Equality (CCE), and its recent donation of "Eyes on the Prize," a Civil Rights documentary film, to the public library. CCE also, the caption states, sponsored an exhibition in a display case at the Page Public Library.[10] It struck me that perhaps this group was involved with the auction block and its dedication, so I sought out members to interview.

The CCE, an organization of approximately twenty individuals consisting of whites, African Americans, and one Hispanic meet informally and irregularly. One member, a white minister, agreed to talk with me and explained what prompted the start of this type of group. Once again I was referred to the news coverage over an event that occurred in 1997, which she named the "catalyzing incident" that brought CCE together.[11] What is important about the formation of CCE is how the group, at first spurred on by racially offensive remarks occurring at a joint Page County Board of Supervisors and School Board meeting, also carried over into a fight over injustice in the heritage arena: members of CCE assisted Frank with the wreath-laying ceremony for the slave auction block.

In late March 1997, during a discussion of consolidating the county's two public high schools, a supervisor made disparaging comments about the U.S.'s immigration policy. The controversy was recounted in the *PN&C*:

'In 1965,' Cubbage said at one point, 'Washington D.C. was a city full of problems. Today it's a city in chaos. You know why? We failed to consider the people who didn't live in the same place we did. . . . We shot a lot of money at the black folks and what did it do for them?' Cubbage continued. 'Nothing. I don't want to see Page County ghettoes in 20 years.'[12]

Cubbage later apologized to the community, but only after citizens decided to meet to discuss the issue and how it could be resolved. From this meeting, the CCE was born.[13]

Cubbage's divisive words, about a white "us" and a black "them" reflects, of course, the segregated physical and cultural landscape of the town, and the exclusion of the African American community in general as active historical agents. Both white and African American citizens were moved not to retaliate, but to figure out how to deal with this public official.

Before their involvement in the slave block dedication, the CCE was also responsible for new displays in one of the most central and often ignored public history sites—the glass case in the public library. According to an informant, they have "broken the chain of library displays" to include African American history.[14] An exhibition devoted to Martin Luther King, Jr., in celebration of his birthday in January, is now a part of the revolving exhibitions here. In January 2000, students from the county's public schools participated in a King celebration sponsored by the CCE. According to a member, "The celebration was bigger than last year, and I hope it will be even bigger next year. . . . It very clearly is well-supported by the whole county."[15] CCE turned a devastating political and racial attack into a mission to support African American history and heritage, as it continued to promote political forums, study circles, and picnics.[16] It may also have been the efforts of the CCE that Christmas wreaths, which are hung on streetlights on the eastern side of Main Street, were put up, for the first time on West Main Street in Christmas 1998. An informant noted to me, however, that the wreaths put up on "The Hill" were old ones.[17]

In the summer of 1999, as I was conducting interviews and researching these heritage issues, another controversy over Confederate history was brewing in Richmond, Virginia. In the construction of the downtown area's Canal Walk, a portrait of Robert E. Lee was exhibited and later taken down because of protests from a City Councilman and local citizens.[18] A compromise was reached, and Lee appeared on the Walk alongside an African American Union soldier and Abraham Lincoln. In January 2000, however, Lee's portrait was vandalized and destroyed.

The battles over the Southern Cross flag, plaguing the nation, are, of course, yet to be resolved, and receive national and local press coverage. An editorial in the *PN&C* on these controversies provided a tendentious perspective on the debate and the City Councilman in Richmond who is vehemently opposed to Lee's portrait:

El-Amin's continuing attack on Lee is a hateful and slanderous lie. So the media is really giving publicity to a smear campaign led by a near comic radical who, for reasons all too obvious, wants to defame and destroy a man who has been and will remain a hero to millions of Americans.[19]

Lee, in this scandal, is not only a hero, but also a victim under siege, under "attack."

Making no bones about his position on this issue, the editor vilified African American Councilman Sa'ad El-Amin: "By the way, El-Amin also says blacks have been 'conditioned,' as one newspaper put it, to 'suppress their feelings' about the white establishment, an ironic statement considering that such 'conditioning' apparently has not worked on El-Amin, although one wishes it had."[20] As harsh as this comment may be, it is also revealing: it shows how discourse on a seemingly innocuous level (through a weekly newspaper) can legitimize a landscape of exclusion.

This type of support for Confederate "heroes," especially Robert E. Lee, was common with my white informants. Those who support Lee's memory, for example, wanted his defacing to be considered a hate crime, and believe Confederate heritage is being ambushed by African Americans who have alternative notions of heritage. A white informant told why he was proud of his southern heritage and why he flew the Southern Cross flag on the roof of his shop (A=author, I=informant):

A: You do have a Confederate flag on your roof. Do you have a special tie to the Confederacy or southern heritage?

I: Southern heritage. And I do it because I think everybody's being morally intimidated away from showing their heritage. You show a flag and some people try to accuse you of being Adolf Hitler, a racist or something. You'd have to look long and hard to find out if I was ever unfair to anybody.

A: So you know about all the controversy . . . there's the thing going on with Lee and his picture in Richmond.

I: They should have gone ahead and done it. See we had a guy here writing letters to the paper and every time he writes one I let him have it.

A: Do you write back?

I: I wrote back.

A: Do you think there could ever be a way to solve all of this?

I: The only way to do it is to not be ashamed of it.

A: You have a relationship to history here because you're a member of the Heritage Association. Why did you decide to become a member?

I: Just to support them. I don't go to the meetings or anything . . . but I think our heritage is under attack.

A: What do you mean by your heritage is under attack?

I: Well, the blacks.

A: You mean your southern heritage? So the reason why you joined is because you want to preserve that?

I: Preserve the good things.

A: And by good things you mean your heritage?

I: Yes, duty, honor.[21]

The rather circular argument, due in large part to my unease about my informant's remarks, shows, once again, how some Confederate supporters have positioned themselves on the defensive with insinuations that criticism of Confederate memory is equated with "moral intimidation." This defensive stance is also evident in expressions for the Civil War as the "War for Southern Independence" and the "War of Northern Aggression." Many of my white informants who supported Confederate heritage used these phrases when expressing their views that Frank's actions at the slave block dedication and remarks in the *PN&C* before the event were derisive.

Frank's initial letter in the *PN&C*, appearing a little over a month before the Confederate statue dedication, warned that the upcoming event was going to be a celebration of the "darkest period in American history." He wrote,

> While the bands are playing 'Dixie' and the Confederate Stars & Bars 'yet wave, an urgent occasion presents itself for all of the county's black churches to come together and give thanks unto God for his deliverance of our race from the depths of slavery and the subsequent decades of beatings, burnings, lynchings, and racial repression that was and is our black 'Confederate heritage.'[22]

In the following two weeks, the editorial section was filled with responses to Frank's letter:

> It is unlikely Barbee had the ideological, cultural, and economic causes of the war in mind as he labored on his masterpiece.[23]

> It was myth that Confederates went to the battlefield to perpetuate slavery. They fought and died because their homeland was invaded and their natural instinct was to protect home and hearth.[24]

> The statue is of a man who fought for his state like many did and for no more reason than that.[25]

> If anything undoes advances blacks have made, it won't be a Confederate gala held once every hundred years. It will be something else that trips them up.[26]

Frank's letter unlocked the floodgates of issues of Confederate heritage, and race relations that have been plaguing southern communities for well over one hundred years. The range of comments suggests that heritage and public history in the south are divided along racial lines. Sanford Levinson writes,

> Sacred grounds characteristically serve as venues for public art, including monuments to social heroes. Yet a sometimes better reality about life within truly multicultural societies is that the very notion of a unified public is up for grabs. As already suggested, one aspect of multiculturalism is precisely that different cultures are likely to have disparate—and even conflicting—notions of who counts as heroes or villains.[27]

Notions of heritage differ not just from group to group or race to race, but person to person. In the first editorial, the Barbee statue is simply a work of art, removed from any political implications. The second and third writers, like many supporters of Confederate heritage, whether it is in support of the Southern Cross flag or a portrait of Robert E. Lee remaining in a prominent position, often use the argument that slavery was not why ordinary soldiers fought in the Civil War. The last writer uses the controversy of the slave block to make a more general comment on race in American history. This episode, then, speaks not just of feuds over ownership to history and heritage, or over debates of who are the heroes and villains, but how race relations and tensions define American history and public history.

Responding to criticism about its sanitized version of pre-Revolutionary America, Colonial Williamsburg now includes a program, "Enslaving America." The living history skits candidly portray some of the mental horrors of slavery: in one, an enslaved couple debates an escape attempt. In another, a group of African American men are told to break up their meeting because of a rule prohibiting more than five blacks to gather in one place.[28] These ambitious and potentially risky programs have received positive feedback from many African American and white visitors, and even the NAACP.[29] But what is perhaps most telling is the effect of programs on Williamsburg's visitors, both black and white. The injustices exhibited have prompted visitors to stop skits by jumping into scenes, trying to stop white actors from playing the roles of slave patrols. Visiting children have followed a black actor throughout the park, in efforts to protect him, after the skit was over.[30]

Black and white visitors, however, interpret colonial slave history differently. Park officials report that, "Although both groups unite in hissing at the slave patrol, whites tend to view the depictions as relics of the past while blacks draw comparisons to the present."[31] Race relations portrayed in the program, including African Americans gathered on city street corners and looked at with suspicion from whites, are still relevant today: where whites may see past injustices, African Americans see contemporary prejudice.

The ways in which history is viewed on personal, community, national, and racial levels is explored in Roy Rosenzweig's and David Thelen's *The Presence of the Past: Popular Uses of History in American Life*. Based on a survey taken with 1,500 Americans, the authors discovered that whites and African Americans do not necessarily share the same ideas about history, especially how it relates to both groups on personal levels. They observed that African Americans were far more likely to defer to a "we," a collective pronoun, when describing the importance of history, family, and historical figures in their lives; whites, on the other hand, most often used "I."[32] Further, African Americans, unlike whites, mentioned the influence of more general historical figures, especially Martin Luther King, Jr., in their lives; whites, described more "intimate tales—how we learned self-reliance during World War II, for example. In the black narratives, famous people and events figured much more centrally."[33] And in visiting public history sites, such as museums, African Americans revealed that they had a more intimate and personal relationship to the history event or person exhibited and interpreted there than whites. Rosenzweig and Thelen claim, "Black respondents tended to directly connect their personal and family narratives to the specific public historical narratives that these sites presented."[34]

Differences in how history is viewed and experienced between whites and African Americans is an egregiously overlooked subject in studying American history. Why do differences exist? As I discussed in chapter one, looking specifically at the difference between the preserved white schoolhouse and the abandoned African American schoolhouse, white public history sites often promote nostalgic views of history and exhibit conflict-free, romanticized pasts. African American history cannot be interpreted in the same way since this past comprises the legacy of slavery. Slavery, however, did not prevent African Americans from creating commemorative events. On January 1, 1808 northern African Americans began to publicly celebrate not the New Year, but the abolition of the slave trade.

These early events were based in African churches, and participants sang, prayed, and listened to a reading of the Congressional Act of Abolition.[35] July 5th celebrations began in 1827 as forums to commemorate state emancipations, and in opposition to white commemorations of freedom.[36] These services were also centered in black churches, but began to move out of these private spaces and into the public eye. According to Genevieve Fabre:

> The transition from the more secret, sacred space of the black church to the streets of major cities created a dramatic change and accounts for the transformation of celebrations. They became more of a community affair and were no longer placed exclusively under the control of the church; they sought more deliberately to attract the attention of white people.[37]

Historian Gregg Kimball also looks at African American expressions of heritage throughout the nineteenth century. He argues that within post-emancipation culture in Virginia, African Americans composed and maintained networks of clandestine oral narratives, whether they were songs or stories "born out of a shared experience of oppression."[38] In Richmond, Virginia, in the year immediately following the Civil War, an African American organization printed and posted a broadside with the following pronouncement, "Notice! The Coloured People of the City of Richmond Would Most Respectfully Inform the Public That THEY DO NOT INTEND To Celebrate THE FAILURE OF THE SOUTHERN CONFEDERACY. . . ."[39] The need to separate out meanings of the outcome of the Civil War and what it symbolized for African Americans as opposed to white southerners arose, then, just after the war.

Earlier, in antebellum Virginia, songs and stories dedicated to Gabriel—an insurrectionist executed for planning a slave revolt—allowed Gabriel's memory to pass through communities and through time. Tellingly, however, multiple versions of the song existed: one rendition was sung away from whites and celebrated black heritage.[40] The other version was sung in the presence of whites for their entertainment and was "a cautionary tale of failure and repression" meant to quell any white fears of future rebellions.[41] Kimball elaborates on the complex expression of African American commemorative activities:

> . . . those under domination may appear in the public realm to be subservient to the system that oppresses them. But, he argues, there is a 'hidden transcript' of resistance created among the oppressed that sometimes peeks out from behind the façade of conformity. Moreover, those thought to be 'powerless' often find ingenious ways to affect the 'public transcript.'[42]

Thus, African American heritage has a tradition of privacy, resistance, and oral transmission. In Luray, however, I discovered that oral history is not a "legitimate" form of history, according to white informants and a prominent white historian: Most of my white informants relegated Frank's actions surrounding the block as embarrassing, irrelevant, and wrongheaded because the history of it is based on oral history. During my fieldwork I attempted to convince a historian, responsible for the erection of Civil War Trails markers, to consider working with the African American community in Page County. While agreeable, he insisted that markers have to be based on fact, not oral history, acknowledging that the history of the slave auction block is not, literally, set in stone. Because the block is surrounded by personal stories, and cannot be verified as an actual block, claims the historian, it is not worth saving. The same standard is followed by the Virginia Department of Historic

Resources and the Civil War Trails program. By basing public history on hard "facts," alternative forms of history are excluded, especially African American ones. Thus the insistence on documents reifies the power structure, as explored in chapter two.

What remains in Luray and towns and cities across America are sculptures, monuments, and other sites centered on white historical actors in a landscape of exclusion. Ironically, as Rosenzweig and Thelen discover in their survey, African Americans, much more so than white Americans, chose a public figure when asked about a person in the past who had especially affected them. Again, whites most often chose a family member.[43] African Americans also discussed "pilgrimages to black shrines" such as the Martin Luther King museum in Memphis, Tennessee.[44] African Americans do not have, however, many places in which to go to learn about and experience their heritage.

Because of a heightened drive to include African Americans and other marginalized communities on the public landscape in the last twenty years, more and more sites dedicated to African American culture will dot the landscape. But will they adequately reflect an African American experience? Simply designating a site as historic—the basis for most of our commemorative landscapes—is most often practiced in very public settings. Since African American heritage traditions are found in more private settings, perhaps the assumptions that tangible, visible sites are the only spaces that represent history and heritage need to be challenged. Genevieve Fabre asserts that African American history should be seen as consisting of *lieux de memoire*, or sites tangible and ephemeral that "are the products of the interaction between history and memory, of the interplay between the personal and the collective."[45] *Lieux de memoire* can be songs, churches, cities, or even the entire Civil Rights Movement. Seen in this way, African American history and its potential to be made public should be studied through a diverse range of sources and methodologies, including as my study demonstrates, ethnography combined with cultural landscape study.

Frank told me that the *PN&C* will print the news the African American community gives to it, and this is, often, not very much. Importantly, too, as my chief African American informant, Frank works virtually alone in his recognition of heritage efforts. He writes off the indifference African Americans have to recapturing heritage to fear and on African Americans having to concentrate more on simply surviving economically.[46]

Perhaps the most recognized heritage event in Luray for African Americans is the annual August celebration of the New York-Virginia Club, a predominantly African American, but racially mixed group commemorating the migration of many of Luray's citizens to cities and other destinations along the eastern seaboard. First organized in 1946, the club, described as "part social, part service organization," celebrates a weeklong reunion, which includes church services, a block party, dance, and picnic, a homecoming for family and friends.[47] As well-established as the group is, they are reluctant, according to an informant, to get involved in preservation activities, preferring to concentrate more on familial relationships. But the celebrations of the New York-Virginia Club also include celebrations vital to the African American community here—church homecomings. An informant described them this way:

> Black homecomings generally follow the same scenario. Folks migrate north and west, gain better employment, educate their kids, mature toward retirement age, get nostalgia for home, and come back to be among old friends. The church is usually the center of most Black communities. It's where the anchoring parents and grand parents and great grand parents, the anchoring "roots" of a family, are based. That's why "homecomings" are often centered around the community church. You know, I've never really heard of a Black homecoming in the north. I think that they were and are a natural progression peculiar to the Black migrations to the north and west away from a repressive south.[48]

Today the African American community celebrates these homecomings in institutions vital to them—churches, some of them historic structures. As Wanda Jackson, a former president and now an active member of the New York-Virginia Club comments, the church "is the central part of the New York-Virginia Club's homecoming."[49] In August 2000, Mount Carmel Baptist Church, built in 1897, celebrated the 50th anniversary of its homecoming services. According to the pastor of the church, these celebrations help to define African American culture, and they are "joyous and serve as a link to heritage."[50] For Wanda Jackson, homecomings, above all, celebrate the "legacy of [our] parents," the original migrants.[51] But to ensure that the tradition will not be lost, the New York-Virginia Club also sponsors a children's block dance that occurs later in the homecoming week.

Associated with heritage celebrations since the early nineteenth century, churches can be considered African American public history sites. Where white commemorative sites are much more likely to be historic homes, monuments, and museums, African Americans often celebrate heritage through services and performances in churches. Publicly designating a church and the events held inside it, however, may jeopardize its private space. On several occasions I was asked to participate in church services and felt that I was intruding on personal and community expressions of faith and heritage. Thus, perhaps certain African American heritage events should remain private to ensure their cultural preservation. I am hopeful that these important and complex issues will be explored by public history practitioners in the future as more and more African American history sites appear on the American landscape.

I needed, though, to explore the history of the block in the community, through its people, and I needed to start with the individual who dedicated it—Frank. To say that I was nervous in meeting Frank is an understatement. Not only was I new to the town and did not know many people, but I was going to speak with someone, whom I was told, was quite outspoken. After many inquiries made to Frank and several white informants about other African Americans involved with heritage, I came up with no one. Frank was also the only African American in Luray who was involved with the dedication of the block and pursuing African American public history. Having lived in Luray most of his adult life, Frank has always been interested in history and is very involved in his church—he leads a gospel choir. He also has a leadership role with African Americans in Luray because of his affiliation with the local NAACP chapter, his involvement with CCE, and his dedication to commemorating the slave block. Members of the African American community in Luray will sometimes come to Frank with complaints of racial bias in hopes that he might bring these to the NAACP.

Our first conversation was uncomfortable but productive for me. He described to me why he wanted to counter-commemorate:

> I'd shit if I were put up on a slave block for the white folks to gawk at, prod, poke, and laugh at before being sold to the highest bidder. I'd certainly have tears if my mother, sister, my child, father, close friend or anyone I'd loved all my life was being sold away right before my eyes—into an unknown, often cruel fate—never to be seen or heard from again. The tears, the urine, the feces, the sweat, the vomit have all long been washed away along with the memories of all those literally millions of black people that shed them on an auction block somewhere. But the "BLOOD" wherever it was shed, still remains. What does it say in Genesis when the Lord questions Cain about Abel "The voice of thy brother's blood cries out to me from the ground." It will NOT be denied. That's how powerful and important this slave auction block is to me.[52]

As I pursued the history of the slave block, and African American history, Frank agreed to help me meet members of the African American community. The day I met up with him to get a ride to visit a couple of informants, Frank told me that we needed to take his tinted-window van because he didn't want people seeing him with me; he insisted that my white informants might not be open with me if they discovered me with him. Astonished, and thinking this was not the deep South during the violent civil rights struggles, I felt he was overreacting. In my view, traveling in a van with a near stranger into a community to which I obviously didn't belong was frightening.

But as my interviews increased and I became bolder with questions regarding the controversy, I understood why Frank wanted me to be hidden for both of our sakes. One of my white informants who flies a Southern Cross flag on his roof told me that he was proud that he looked like Nathan Bedford Forrest, the founder of the Ku Klux Klan. He asked about the resemblance, pointing out Forrest's picture front and center on his mantelpiece. There were also vague and frightening phrases such as "there's a good old boy network here and they want their history exhibited, no one else's."[53] What also disturbed me was how many of my white informants just assumed that I didn't know Frank or were aware of how he felt. Instead, they spoke openly and honestly with me in ways they wouldn't have if they had known I was friends with him. I guessed that as a white person, I was now a part of a white allegiance and could be trusted with whites' "truths" about history in Luray. What I discovered is that Frank knew this, and why I had to remain hidden in his van if I wanted to keep this double agency going.

I also realized that the traditional ethnographic equation of "us" and "them" was shattered on several levels. First, I had to acknowledge that there was another "us" and "them" within Luray itself—whites and African Americans. Second, I was an outsider, of course, but I felt it was necessary to at times be an "us" and a "them" depending on the race and heritage sentiments of my informants. A white informant disclosed disturbing information to me—an experience about a deliberate act of racism—and she asked that I not discuss the issue with African American informants out of respect for them. I also somewhat secretly attended meetings sponsored by white southern heritage groups, not wanting to jeopardize my status within the white community.

Ethnography also forced me to look beyond simplistic oppositions when pursuing the history and significance of the block: not all African Americans in Luray support or believe the block was used to sell slaves and not all whites have attended Confederate heritage events at the Confederate soldier monuments. If I had simply pursued a cultural landscape study focused only on the commemorative landscape and primary research, I never would have realized the multidimensionality of these public history sites and how deeply race relations are embedded in this stone block and in the representation of the community. Thus, ethnography can help start dialogues on race and public history, maybe a first step toward a more equitable historical representation in narratives and the landscape in Luray.

The fact that a slave block was dedicated as a piece of public history in a town devoted to Confederate memory is significant, of course, but the date on which it occurred, the day of the rededication of the Herbert Barbee Confederate soldier statue, is perhaps even more significant. This block stood in direct opposition to the Confederate heritage that was being celebrated on a large scale that day, with the racial and political resonances taking on even greater importance. According to Frank, he placed the wreath on the block the morning of the Confederate celebration and remained next to the block and wreath during the course of the event. People who attended the Confederate ceremony discussed the possibility of the block being used to sell slaves, but also told him it was most likely a stepping stone for mounting horses or climbing into carriages.

Even though the block has been neglected throughout its history, it still subverted dominant notions of heritage on its dedication day and even today. David Lowenthal argues that, "Heritage exaggerates and omits, candidly invents and frankly forgets, and thrives on ignorance and error."[54] In the previous chapters I have illuminated Lowenthal's claim by exposing the exclusionary heritage practices in Luray. But heritage, as demonstrated through the auction block, can also serve to candidly reinvent and frankly remember marginalized cultures.

The block is the only piece of public history in Luray to suggest an alternative past. As such, the heritage embodied in it is a necessary and vital way to challenge dominant notions of memory and heritage, just as the early nineteenth century African American heritage celebrations sought to assert emerging African American notions of memory. In their provocative article, "Artifacts as Expressions of Society and Culture: Subversive Genealogy and the Value of History," Mark Leone and Barbara Little suggest that "self-justifying genealogies" are tools by which an individual or state asserts certain ideologies which appear to be "natural" or historically inevitable. In their study, they examine Charles Wilson Peale's natural history museum and the Maryland State House, two works of the Federal Era.[55] They illuminate their claim:

> Knowledge of history provides the power to create genealogy, and such power is the key to control. Genealogy here is to be seen as the version of history that suggests the inevitability of the present social order. Thus genealogy becomes a political necessity because it legitimizes the tie between the present and the past. . . . Connections between past and present are inevitable, determined, or epigenetic, implying that the present could not be other than it is.[56]

One of the genealogies at work in Luray is the Confederate history of the Civil War, and the artifacts, statues, road signs, and celebrations all serve to make these historical moments the most important in the town's history. This commemorative hegemony leaves no room for alternative, or subversive genealogies, unless they happen to be discovered on the landscape. In Luray, the dedication of the slave auction block provided this subversive story revealing how material culture and public material culture can illuminate the study of history and memory.

The auction block can also represent how one artifact can elicit perspectives and emotions based on race and individual and communal notions of heritage, and the profound differences in these perspectives derived from objects on the American landscape. Certainly one of the most contested history sites revolving around the differences between black and white perspectives on slavery is the John Brown Fort, the site of the unsuccessful slave revolt in 1859 in Harper's Ferry, West Virginia. After Reconstruction and during the Jim Crow era, the site became one of the few where African Americans could visit an actual *place* devoted to their years of horrific servitude and to celebrate John Brown's determination to abolish slavery.[57]

Thus, the block and an interrogation of the controversy surrounding it can yield a plethora of information on larger issues including the subversive potential of artifacts in recapturing heritage, differences in white and African American history and memory, the invisibility of African American public history on the American landscape, issues involving race and public history, and race as a factor in the ethnographic equation of "us and them." Perhaps most importantly, the slave auction block also demonstrates that heritage—here the acceptance of an alternative history—can be a necessary and dynamic part of gaining agency in the historic process if its goal is cultural inclusion. Possibly inauthentic and ensconced in power relationships, the block can still serve to liberate.

In October 2000, in an unprovoked action, an "antiwreath" and handmade plaque were placed at the slave auction block.[58] The commemorator wrote:

> In Memory. . . . Of days by-gone, days of grace and Manners in the Southland Represented by this symbol called a CARRIAGE STEPPING STONE Which assisted men, women and children to enter and exit a Horse-drawn vehicle. May this rock find peace back in the Quarry [caps his].

The dedicator left his name, apparently wanting to claim responsibility for his actions. A couple of weeks after the random placing of the "antiwreath," a popular Valley historian wrote an article on the role of African Americans in the Confederacy. Arguing that a "significant number" of African Americans fought willingly for the Confederacy, the historian's claims hit a nerve with Frank. He, in turn, wrote an editorial in the following week's *PN & C,* insisting that

> Suppose that for the sake of discussion that hundreds of blacks did flock to the Confederate cause. . . . Suppose they fought for the denial of the most basic human rights for themselves. . . . How, then, were those 'good Negroes' and their progeny rewarded? Through continued and often brutal disenfranchisement in every aspect of Southern society.[59]

And, once again, a rebuttal written by a white informant accused Frank of aggression:

> He [Frank] has attacked Southern heritage and attempted to demonize the entire white population of Page County repeatedly—and seemingly there will be no end to these attacks.[60]

Coincidentally, in the same issue, a historian wrote of slavery in the Valley. The following week Frank once again had a letter printed, this one noting again the inhumane ways the stories of slaves in the Valley are told. He writes

> There are interesting references to factual statistics regarding the number of slaves and slave owners in Page County before the war. The terms 'slave' and 'slavery' appear here, like in other Confederate publications and literature, as objective, abstract, and statistical terms—inconsequential things, primarily devoid of full human value or consideration.[61]

Frank goes on to write that he would like to know more about the lives and emotions of the slaves—how they felt as they were auctioned: "Did he have to leave his wife and children behind? Was he sold on the block at public auction?"[62] Although no rebuttals were in the following issue of the *PN&C*, Frank received, to his surprise, positive feedback at the annual Christmas concert held in the Mauck Meeting House in early December 2000. As they did the following year, as described in chapter two, the choir performed to an all-white, largely PCHA member event. The gospel singing emotionally affected many in the audience, as Frank discovered in comments he received after the show. One woman told Frank she was moved by his letter about slavery in the paper; the president of the PCHA wanted to know if Frank was interested in collaborating on an upcoming show on school segregation in Page County, and another woman was moved by Frank's use of the stomp stick in the performance. She said she was reminded of church services when she was growing up in nearby Fauquier County. She promised Frank she would research the use of the stick and correspond with him.[63]

Frank's persistence to see the block and African American history recognized in Luray, and the resistance of many members of the white community to accept it as a legitimate piece of public history, continues today. The first steps toward reconciliation, which may be occurring, should consist of recognizing our shared heritage and shared public landscapes, as well as seeking out fresh perspectives on the similarities and differences between white and African American conceptions of history, memory, and public history in Luray and in the United States.

NOTES

1. Elizabeth Rauh Bethel, *The Roots of African-American Identity: History and Memory in Antebellum Free Communities* (New York: St. Martin's), 1977.
2. "Looking for Information About Luray's Mysterious Slave Block," *Page News and Courier*, 13 August 1998.
3. Another image of a slave block I have been able to locate sits at Green Hill Plantation in Campbell County, Virginia. From photographs, it appears that the block in Luray could have been a part of a larger structure used to sell slaves.
4. "Looking for Information . . ." *Page News and Courier*, 13 August 1998.
5. Charlie Thomas. Interview by the author. July 1999.
6. "High-Tech Sleuths Study 'Slave Block'" *Page News and Courier*, 23 September 1999, Page County Public Library, Luray, Virginia.
7. Dr. James Starrs et al., "The Slave Auction Block of Luray, Virginia: A Report on the September 18, 1999 Investigation," George Washington University, Department of Forensic Anthropology, Washington, DC.
8. Starrs et al., "The Slave Auction Block Report."
9. Robert H. Moore II, "Did Page County African-Americans Serve for the Confederacy?" *Page News and Courier*, 2 November 2000.
10. "Remembering Dr. King," *Page News and Courier*, 28 January 1999.
11. Gale Curtis. Interview by the author, 22 June 1999.
12. "Cubbage's Words Cause Outrage," *Page News and Courier*, 29 March 1997.
13. "Cubbage's Words Cause Outrage," *Page News and Courier*, 29 March 1997.
14. Gale Curtis. Interview by the author. 22 June 1999.
15. "Students celebrate Dr. King's life," *Page News and Courier*, 20 January 2000, Page County Public Library, Luray, Virginia.
16. Meeting Notes, Concerned Citizens for Equality, 8 July 1999. According to the notes, it was suggested that "we approach . . . the Page County School Board about inviting School Board and/or school personnel to a mini presentation regarding issues of concern, i.e. violence, peer counseling, etc."
17. Gale Curtis. Interview by the author. 22 June 1999.
18. "Robert E. Lee: Saint or Sinner?" *Richmond Times-Dispatch*, 27 July 1999.
19. "Lee Embattled Again," *Page News and Courier*, 22 July 1999, Page County Public Library, Luray, Virginia.
20. "Lee Embattled Again."
21. Richard Sandler. Interview by the author. 22 June 1999.
22. "Celebration of Confederate Statue Hurts Racial Harmony," *Page News and Courier*, 18 June 1998, editorial.
23. "Heritage Event Not a 'Cause,'" *Page News and Courier*, 25 June 1998, editorial.
24. "Myths About Civil War Are Many," *Page News and Courier*, 2 July 1998, editorial.
25. "Statue Not About White Supremacy," *Page News and Courier*, 2 July 1998, editorial.
26. "Statue Not About White Supremacy."

27. Sanford Levinson, *Written in Stone: Public Monuments in Changing Societies* (Durham, NC: Duke University Press, 1998), 37.

28. "A Taste of Slavery Has Tourists Up in Arms: Williamsburg's New Skits Elicit Raw Emotions," *The Washington Post*, 7 July 1999.

29. "A Taste of Slavery."

30. "A Taste of Slavery."

31. "A Taste of Slavery."

32. Roy Rosenzweig and David Thelen, *The Presence of the Past: Popular Uses of History in American Life* (New York, Columbia University Press, 1998), 150.

33. Rosenzweig and Thelen, *The Presence of the Past*, 152.

34. Rosenzweig and Thelen, *The Presence of the Past,* 155.

35. Genevieve Fabre, "African-American Commemorative Celebrations in the Nineteenth Century" in Genevieve Fabre and Robert O'Meally, eds., *History & Memory in African American Culture* (New York: Oxford University Press, 1994), 78.

36. Fabre, "African-American Commemorative Celebrations."

37. Fabre, "African-American Commemorative Celebrations."

38. Gregg Kimball, "African, American, and Virginian": The Shaping of Black Memory in Antebellum Virginia, 1790–1860, in W. Fitzhugh Brundage, ed., *Where These Memories Grow: History, Memory, and Southern Identity* (Chapel Hill: University of North Carolina Press, 2000), 59.

39. Kammen, 122.

40. Kimball, "African, American, and Virginian," 62.

41. Kimball, "African, American, and Virginian," 62.

42. Kimball, "African, American, and Virginian," 58.

43. Rosenzweig and Thelen, *The Presence of the Past*, 153.

44. Rosenzweig and Thelen, *The Presence of the Past*, 155.

45. Genevieve Fabre and Robert O'Meally, *History and Memory in African American Culture*, 7.

46. Frank Hall. E-mail to the author. November 1999.

47. "Extended Family: 'New York-Virginia' Club Draws from Everywhere in Between," *Page News and Courier*, 31 August 2000.

48. Frank Hall. Email to the author, 3 September 2000.

49. Wanda Jackson. Interview by the author. 24 July 2001.

50. "Mount Carmel Baptist Celebrates 'Golden' Homecoming," *Page News & Courier*, 24 August 2000.

51. Wanda Jackson. Interview by the author. 24 July 2001.

52. Frank Hart, email to the author, 11 September 1999.

53. Bill Monroe, Interview by the author. July 1999.

54. David Lowenthal, *Possessed by the Past: The Heritage Crusade and the Spoils of History* (New York: The Free Press, 1996), 121.

55. Mark P. Leone and Barbara J. Little, "Artifacts as Expressions of Society and Culture: Subversive Genealogy and the Value of History" in *History from Things: Essays on Material Culture*, Steven Lubar and W. David Kingery, eds. (Washington, DC: Smithsonian Institution Press, 1993), 160–81.

56. Leone and Little, "Artifacts as Expressions," 173.

57. Paul A. Shackel, *Memory in Black and White: Race, Commemoration, and the Post-Bellum Landscape* (AltaMira Press, 2003): 73.

58. My informant Frank and I gave this name to the wreath.

59. "Black Confederates Never Included in Southern Society," *Page News & Courier*, 9 November 2000.

60. "—— Writes With a One-Track Mind" *Page News & Courier*, 16 November 2000.

61. "History Dehumanizes Slaves," *Page News and Courier*, 22 November 2000.

62. "History Dehumanizes Slaves."

63. Frank Hall. E-mail to the author. December 2000.

Chapter Four

Tourism and Battles for Cultural Identity

In *Touring the Shenandoah Valley Backroads*, a picture of a structure, "The Old Gazebo in Hamburg" rests on the side lawn of Calendine, famed Luray sculptor Herbert Barbee's historic home. This structure is actually a part of a bell tower, removed in 1994 from Mt. Carmel Primitive Baptist Church in downtown Luray because it was thought to be unstable in high winds. A rare example of Greek Revival architecture, the structure is nearly one hundred years old and it cost the PCHA $800.00 to have it moved to its present home.

The bell tower (or gazebo) holds a special importance for Luray's citizens, and particularly the Heritage Association. Not wanting to see it destroyed, and not concerned that it may look a little odd resting on the grass, PCHA saved a piece of heritage that is not necessarily meant for the tourist's eye. Just how much Luray and other communities decide to reveal about their history and identity to tourists is an important element to this study, and is a significant and dynamic aspect to studying tourism. In Luray, I discovered that the relationship the locals have and have had with tourists since the latter nineteenth century is not a one-sided and one-dimensional host and guest relationship; it is a dynamic interplay between tourists, including African Americans, a neglected population in tourism study, locals, vendors, cooperation, resistance, cultural identity, notions of heritage, and profit.

In this chapter, I present an overview of the history of tourism in Luray and the nearby Shenandoah National Park (SNP), especially in its early years, and look at its status today. I argue that although Luray and the neighboring mountain community saw thousands of visitors in the late nineteenth and early twentieth centuries, including tourists, sociologists, missionaries, craft school teachers, and government officials, and they continue to see large numbers of tourists today, they were and are able to resist commodification and sustain their own ideas and practices of heritage within a larger Shenandoah Valley framework of Civil War and Confederate heritage practices. This resistance is noteworthy since other indigenous cultures in Appalachia have a history of being exploited as "folk"—as a romanticized people whose national significance lay in their ability to produce handmade crafts for middle- and upper-class Americans. This constructed image and commodification, which Luray has avoided, transformed both cultural identities and the landscape in the Appalachian region in the late nineteenth and early twentieth centuries.

Heritage celebrations in Luray, as I have demonstrated, have centered on Civil War and Confederate memory, which pervade the entire Shenandoah Valley. But Luray is one of the few areas of the Valley with two Confederate soldier monuments as town centerpieces, and where commemorations focused on these statues have such a long and community supported tradition. Town officials and citizens, however, also want to integrate Luray's distinct relationship with Confederate heritage into larger Civil War commemorative efforts in the Valley, especially the Virginia Civil War Trails Project.

Today, the Project, which helps communities designate "important" areas of Civil War history for promoting heritage preservation and tourism, is well supported by historians, heritage groups, and many white citizens in Luray. But as more and more historical markers bring attention to Civil War skirmishes, the history presented to tourists and citizens is a static interpretation of the landscape and the people who once lived on it. What is lacking in this interpretation, I argue, is a perspective of the people of Civil War Virginia— of the day-to-day life of soldiers, women, and African Americans—all groups who are central to an understanding of the Civil War. Instead, as a recent community study on Civil War interpretation reveals, citizen groups in the Valley wish to create and sustain standard interpretations of the Civil War in visitor centers and public history sites. These include a thematic framework of "The Valley, The Campaigns, and The Battlefields" established by the Shenandoah Valley Battlefields National Historic District Commission.[1]

The first tourists to Luray sought out the Luray Caverns to experience the sublime underground landscapes, and Skyland, a late eighteenth-century Victorian resort located in the Blue Ridge Mountains that hosted wealthy Northern Virginians and Washingtonians and employed Luray citizens (including African Americans), and mountain people. Run by George Freeman Pollock, a wealthy Washingtonian and businessman, the vacation spot saw cultures collide as hosts and guests interacted and negotiated space, power, and cultural identity. A look at Skyland reveals that even though Luray's citizens and the mountain people were affected by the tourist trade, they used the experience for economic gain: Evidence shows that both Luray citizens and mountain people hosted and even housed overnight guests. Therefore, the relationship that Pollock and the tourists shared cannot simply be understood as exploitative—a common theme in tourism scholarship.

When Pollock's resort was torn down to establish the Shenandoah National Park in 1935, there were new types of tourists—middle-class whites and even African Americans traveling to the Blue Ridge and the Valley. For the most part, Luray supported the Park in terms of income potential, and even the mountain people, who were removed from their homes to make way for the Park, entertained and sold crafts to tourists.

The Park's early years, however, were somewhat tumultuous as the challenges of the displaced mountain families had to be met, and as African Americans came to experience the beauty and recreation of the mountains in a segregated state and segregated park. African American travelers and tourists, although they were consigned to marginalized tourist spaces, including a segregated campsite and tourist cabins, visited the Park in large numbers and were responsible for integration in the Park years before other similar sites in Virginia.

While white Luray citizens have held heritage celebrations and actively negotiated tourism, African American citizens were and are forced to negotiate on completely different terms: they could only visit, eat, and stay in certain places, and were forced to stay in remote and segregated areas outside of town. African Americans, as tourists, battled separate and unequal treatment. I look at the history of African American tourism here, interrogate tourism literature and argue that the history of tourism must be considered along racial lines in Luray and elsewhere around the world.

Finally, I assert that the group of outsiders who present the greatest threat to the town's identity today are the recent influx of retirees and transplants who have moved into the area from eastern urban and suburban areas. These "postmodern" tourists are threatening maybe the most vital aspect of the town's collective identity—its agricultural character. Their presence and the challenges the town is facing as a result of this population help to introduce a provocative topic in the field and expand traditional definitions of tourism. The battles for cultural identity in Luray are not focused on what to do with the tourists who stay for a day or two, but what to do with these outsiders who stay permanently and their desires to "change things," as some of my informants told me.

As I look at tourism in Luray, my guiding paradigm centers on ideas developed by anthropologist Quetzil Castaneda. In his turgid, yet fresh overview of ethnography and tourism, *In the Museum of Maya Culture: Touring Chichen Itza*, Castaneda argues that tourism's "impact" does not exist; instead, tourism is an amalgam of the "politics of identity construed at regional, national, local, and international levels."[2] Further, "impact" implies a one-sided study, usually focused on the *results* of tourism, and ignores the "impacted" culture's role in an ethnographic equation. Instead, Castaneda believes, tourism should be studied as a "long history of interaction, collusion, mutual influence, and even opposition."[3] This much more dynamic perspective, looking at tourism as continually contested and negotiated, fits the situation in Luray remarkably. The community's resistance to commodification, their steadfast tradition of heritage celebrations, and their refusal to yield to the newest group of outsiders is evidence of a strong, albeit conservative cultural identity. Although it can be argued that some of this resistance may actually be economically harmful to the community, the citizens, nonetheless, have been willing and able to resist and accept impact, proving that Castaneda's ideas can lay the foundation for more nuanced and diversified studies of tourism in local communities. Instead of depending on the paradigm of host vs. guest and the inevitability of host exploitation caused by mass tourism, tourism scholarship now embraces a much more multifaceted view of tourism. As Erve Chambers writes,

> It is important to recognize that these mediations [between host and guest] do not invariably imply negative consequences for the communities associated with tourism. Neither are the ideologies associated with modern tourism of a single kind—the imposition of tourist resorts and theme parks, urban revitalization efforts, ecotourism, and even attempts to counter the effects of mass tourism with 'sustainable,' community-based tourism initiatives—all of these represent varieties of dominance to the extent that they seek their particular ends by attempting to control the terms by which the tourism experience is defined.[4]

In the last twenty-five years or so, Chambers, Casteneda, and other tourism scholars have called for new and expanded definitions of tourism and tourists, including deconstructing the power structures endemic to tourist/host relationships. I attempt, as well, to look beyond the statistics into the interplay of how different groups in Luray have negotiated history, public history, identity, and tourism and how and why the public history the tourists see is defined largely in terms of power struggles.

Discovered accidentally in 1878 by Benton Stebbins, a tinsmith and a photographer, the Luray Caverns were largely responsible for bringing the first tourists en masse to Luray. Caves, however, had already been established as tourist destinations in the area: Grand Caverns, located south of the Rockingham-Augusta county line (approximately 40 miles south of Luray), opened to travelers as early as 1806.[5]

Fueled by the coming of the railroad, Luray became an upper-class tourist destination. By the early part of the twentieth century and with a rising middle class and the promotion of the natural world as tourist destinations, Luray drew thousands to its hotels and inns, some of which lined Main Street, including the Luray Cave Hotel. The ornate and Victorian Luray Inn was situated atop what is now Inn-Lawn Park, just up the hill from the train depot. In 1921, for example, 10,000 New Yorkers visited the Caverns, setting an attendance record.[6]

Leisure travel and tourism, having their roots in the latter eighteenth century, coincided with a burgeoning consumerism and the increased desire to have new and better things. Travel and tourism enabled people to be fashionable by being seen in the places to be seen, and traveling and enjoying time in the "in" parts of late nineteenth century America. As roads improved, the population grew, and agricultural, industrial, and commercial developments expanded the economy of the new world and the possibilities of travel for all levels of society; the need to "keep up with the Joneses" even on their vacations become more apparent and more important.[7]

The emergence of a "tame" landscape, which helped fuel the tourism trade in Luray, can be linked to the beginning of landscape painting and ultimately to a shift in the perception of landscape beginning in the late eighteenth century. The Romantic worldview, prominent with thinkers, artists, and writers between 1790–1830, helped to change how nature was seen and represented. Where Enlightenment thinkers conceptualized nature in more holistic and rational ways, the Romantics stressed an individual's unique and emotional attachment to the natural world: "The Romantics recognized that beautiful scenery elevated the feelings—particularly when it evoked solitude and awe. . . . Nature became the religion of many, and the forest became the church."[8] Thus, Luray Caverns, which would have been considered "sublime" maybe fifty years beforehand, was now a tame underground landscape offering an escape from modernity.[9] Indeed, the fact that some of the natural formations in the Caverns were named for what they resembled, that is, a section of stalactites hanging like fish was called the "fish market,"[10] reveals that this underground landscape was being tamed to suit the public (figure 9). Today, during a tour, the guide will still point out these formations.

Not all visitors to Luray simply took in the amazing natural sights; some, even at this early date, pondered the effects of tourism on the local culture. Shortly after the discovery of the Caverns, Stebbins invited reporters, artists, and scholars to examine the Caverns first hand. One writer, science professor

Figure 9.   Luray Caverns

Jerome J. Collins from the *New York Herald*, worried about the Caverns's effect on the locals:

> 'Ah, Sir,' said an old resident, 'If we only had a railroad here what a fine thing this cave would be for Luray.' . . . Sure enough, it would help things amazingly, but I fear the material benefits to be enjoyed would be counter-balanced by moral evils that would change a kind-hearted, hospitable, courteous, and honest community into a race of boarding house harpies.[11]

Collins's comments reflect a socially constructed image of the Valley culture that is still prevalent today: that the people embody pre-capitalist virtues and could potentially become corrupted by tourism development. But Collins also reveals that local citizens were a part of a tourist's experience in Luray—that they were attractions as well. A similar cultural image of native Nantucketers was constructed in the late 1800s. As Dona Brown writes, "But outsiders were often not so much interested in historical landmarks as they were in the *people* of the island, whom they often imagined as historical relics themselves."[12]

As the word spread beyond the mountains of a culture supposedly immune to the alienating effects of city life, the demand to visit these areas, and to buy the goods made by the mountain people burgeoned. In exhibitions in cities and in popular magazines and government reports, news spread of these goods and this culture, perpetuating a stereotype of a romanticized bucolic lifestyle untouched by urban ills.[13]

The early tourism trade in Luray provided an impetus for improving environmental and social standards, and shows how citizens negotiated tourism to use it to the advantage of the community. In 1879 telephone wires were strung above the streets, and the town council passed ordinances prohibiting "swimming in the Hawksbill Creek, loose pigs on the street, fast driving through the town and cows roaming at large after eight o'clock at night."[14] Thus, tourism was transforming the landscape and sparking economic growth, changes that were welcome to the community. In 1881, the *PN&C* reported that citizens raised funds for the chief of police to purchase a new uniform, and that this action "is a move ahead of any neighboring villages and proves Luray to be a progressive town."[15] The Norfolk and Western Railroad built the grand hotel, the Luray Inn, in 1881, accommodating guests from all over the United States and the world. Tourism also helped to expand businesses. In the late 1800s, the Deford Tannery, the largest in the country, was completed, and by 1890, Luray boasted a cigar factory, a flour mill, and a furniture factory.[16]

Luray was on the edge of an economic boom. The Valley Land & Improvement Company, a northern-based speculating firm, bought over 10,000 acres of land around Luray, including the Caverns and the Luray Inn.[17] Unfortunately, few lots were purchased and the company went bankrupt only a year later, a scene not uncommon throughout the Shenandoah Valley. To exacerbate an already tragic situation, the grand Luray Inn burned to the ground in 1891, and the country suffered a national depression in 1893.[18] After these unfortunate events, tourism was never the same in Luray. The failed land ventures, the fire, and the depression brought the tourism rate from 3,000 persons a month in the 1880s to 3,000 per year by the 1890s.[19]

Even in its heyday, Luray Caverns brought more popularity than economic benefits to Luray—a common side effect of tourism on host communities. Those who benefited the most, were, of course, the owners of the Caverns who purchased the land cheaply and were able to sell it years later for enormous profits. As Elizabeth Ann Atwood points out, the 1880s in Luray saw little economic growth, and even decline.[20] Oddly, perhaps, the periods of economic growth were the 1860s and 1890s, times that were tumultuous for many parts of the nation, according to U.S. Census data.

Today, the Luray Caverns Corporation, a private, family-owned operation, owns two hotels, an antique car and carriage museum, a restaurant, a country club, an airport, and the Caverns. The cave itself is valued at over one million dollars.[21] But with all the success of the Caverns even today, Page County is

still suffering economically. Unemployment in 1982, for example, was as
high as 20 percent. Today, it is much lower at approximately two percent, but
still remains slightly higher than the state average.[22] As well, the potential for
the Caverns Company to work with the PCHA in promoting mutual events
has not been fully explored. One of my informants told me that the owning
family simply wants to go about its own business and no one else's.[23]

Tourism in the 1880s led to improvements in the town's image of itself,
even though most people were not benefiting economically from it. Luray citizens were, however, able to retain a strong, Confederate heritage identity by
dedicating the Barbee soldier monument in 1898, occurring at the same time
as tourists were beginning to visit the town. Thus, expressions of regional
identity created through a public monument, or through public history, tell
much about people and places that tourism statistics do not reveal.

In addition to the Luray Caverns, the Civil War—its battles, battlefields,
regiments, cemeteries, and personal stories—is an enormous draw for tourists
to the Shenandoah Valley. In fact, it is so important to tourism here that in
1996, a Congressional act created the Shenandoah Valley Battlefields National
Historic District Commission to "address grassroots concerns in the Valley
about preserving its Civil War heritage and promoting tourism."[24] The Commission is also responsible for considering "'related resources'—individual
sites, buildings, towns, railroads, roads, and landscapes—to weave local and
regional stories together into a cohesive story, meaningful to residents and visitors alike."[25]

The lack of Civil War activity in Page County has proved to be a big dis-
appointment for historians, city officials, and citizens interested in designating historic sites. Because of the absence of actual battles, the Page County
Civil War Commission has decided to concentrate on memorializing sites of
several skirmishes, and erecting Civil War Trails markers as part of the
statewide program. Historians and citizens are hopeful that these sites will
attract tourists. A possible kiosk is also being planned for a spot in the middle of town, Inn Lawn Park. This structure will discuss Page County's role
in the Civil War, and be placed near the slave auction block. Whether or not
it will include a discussion of slavery is a point that will be determined in the
future.

A planning team and the Commission held a "Stakeholders Workshop" in
June 1999, inviting various people associated with tourism, historical interpretation, and economic development in the Valley to share ideas for
tourism development. Many themes were given at this meeting in New
Market, Virginia and at other meetings held in locations in the Valley, with
citizens wanting interpretation to include exploring the "civilian story,"
"old family recipes for authentic 19th century food," and "trains."[26] The
Commission is well on its way to building five "battlefield orientation cen-

ters" in different spots in the Valley. Unfortunately, Luray did not receive one of these centers.

This significant effort is important to this paper because it shows not only that tourism is centered on the Civil War in the Valley, but also how local citizens want tourists to perceive and experience the War. Citizen groups did decide that they wanted interpretation to include day-to-day life, but failed to mention the daily life of African Americans. Rather than discussing slavery or even free black communities, citizens and officials alike wanted more personal stories of wartime, but stories focused on depoliticized topics such as cooking in a nineteenth-century kitchen. At the 8 June 1999 meeting, I suggested an African American theme for inclusion to the other themes called out, which were consequently written down by the meeting's organizers. My suggestion did not get written down. During an intermission period, a representative from a county in the Valley whispered to me, "I know you want to do well, and so do I, but I honestly think I know more about black history than the blacks I've talked to." Somewhat startled, I knew from that point on that the Commission was not interested in including a historical interpretation based on African American history. I thought, why should they when there were no African Americans in the room to begin with?

As a result of these meetings, public history and tourism in the Shenandoah Valley will continue to be centered on the Civil War, and in Luray, if not in many other parts of the Valley, Confederate public history will dominate the commemorative landscapes. The possibility that interpretation for tourists could include a much broader, more inclusive view of the Civil War will be overlooked as it has in the past for honoring the Confederacy, whose interpretation would lose its legitimacy to tourists if it mentioned slavery—an attitude felt by many of my white informants.

Although tourism to the Shenandoah Valley was on the decline at the turn of the century, new national efforts to buy and reserve natural areas for preservation and visitation were on the rise especially due to the birth of the National Park Service in 1916. Yosemite, established in 1872, was this country's first national park, but hopes for an eastern park were not yet met until President Herbert Hoover first brought attention to the natural wonders of the Blue Ridge in the 1920s. Upper-class visitors, however, were already enjoying the Blue Ridge Mountains at Skyland, George Freeman Pollock's ornate resort, just minutes from Luray, and were even treated to dinners in the homes of mountain people.

These dinners, listed in the promotional literature for Skyland, constitute evidence that the citizens of Luray and the mountain people cooperated with Pollack and his tourist venture, proving that even at tourism's earliest stages, tourism "impact" was not one-dimensional and one-directional. Pollack, for example, relied on letters from a Page County resident, John David Printz, who reported on conditions at the resort when Pollack was not there. In the winter of 1893–94, Pollack received a letter from Printz notifying him that:

> high winds and zero weather had made White Oak Canyon more beautiful than it had been in many years. I had been hoping to get some winter pictures of the various waterfalls and was therefore quite excited.[27]

In fact, Printz was a key figure in Skyland's history and establishment: he was the first Luray citizen Pollack met and was instrumental in garnering support from other citizens to help Pollack with his early expedition teams and his tourists. Printz and his colleagues also helped build the cabins at Skyland.[28] Although Pollack did have some problems with the mountain people (drunkenness, stealing), he depended on them to make his business function. Moreover, some of the citizens mentioned in his book had personal relationships with Pollack. He depended on several of Page County's citizens including Printz, Sam Sours, the postal carrier, and Will Grigsby, an African American cook and musician. Pollack also utilized resources in town, from banking with a Luray establishment to buying lumber in a privately owned store. Maybe most importantly in regard to tourism, Pollack arranged to have his expedition team, and later his guests, stay in citizens' homes.[29]

Pollack's employment of African Americans from Blainesville and his invitation for African American gospel groups to sing at his resort reveal the presence of an African American population in Luray and their involvement in the tourist trade here. On July Fourth celebrations, for example, Pollack reported to have "singing, mostly spirituals, by the Negro folks from Blainesville, and clog dancing by other colored people."[30] Pollack's autobiography also contains photographs of African Americans who worked for him including Will Grigsby and his band, a domestic worker named Sadie, and Uncle Bob Mallory, an African American preacher. African American children even appear in a remarkable photo of a "gay outing" in 1895 (figure 10).

The landscape of Skyland that cut across class and racial boundaries was soon turned over to the federal government to create the Shenandoah National Park. The indigenous inhabitants, some of whom worked with Pollock, were scrutinized by sociologists and government officials and forced to undergo intelligence tests and anthropological studies. When the government finally decided to remove them (discussion did ensue over the possibility of leaving them there for the entertainment of the tourists), the only remnant of their way of life was an exhibition mounted in the 1960s in the largest visitor center in the Park. This tendentious exhibition, now replaced by a more equitable representation of the mountain people, is the subject of the next chapter.

In 1932, as planning for the SNP was underway, Arno B. Cammerer, the Deputy Director of the Park Service, was concerned with creating recre-

Figure 10.   Pollock's Party

ational space for African Americans.[31] Harold Ickes, the Secretary of the Interior, was also very concerned with the status of African Americans, pushing for an integrated park. But Virginia's strict segregation laws, and the racist business practices of the concessionaire company for the Park, the Virginia Sky-Line Company, snuffed Ickes's progressive hopes. He did manage, however, to integrate the Pinnacles Picnic Grounds (in the middle section of the park, just east of Luray) as an "experiment," and in 1939, African Americans were consigned to one area of the park, Lewis Mountain, located in the mid-section of the Park, approximately ten miles south of Luray (figure 11). The Park Service named it the "Negro Area."[32]

Ickes's personal integration politics and Virginia's segregationist politics created feuds within the higher echelons of the Park Service. While James Lassiter, the first park superintendent, was recuperating from a heart attack in December 1939, Ickes intervened into the Park's policies and ordered Cammerer to prohibit the mention of segregation in any maps, signage, or promotional materials in the park.[33] When Lassiter returned and discovered Ickes's demands, he criticized the confusing policies. Ickes was ultimately responsible for having Lassiter sent to Santa Fe, New Mexico with a grade cut and a 10 percent salary cut.[34]

Certainly Lassiter was caught between Virginia's segregation laws, the concessionaire's business practices, and Ickes's progressive stance on integration, but according to a business memo, he supported the Virginia Sky-Line Company's refusal to build an African American facility. Purportedly the company was reluctant to provide food and accommodations because it felt there were not enough African American visitors to make it profitable. Evidence suggests,

Figure 11.   Negro Mountain

however, that visitation to the Park and to Lewis Mountain was high in the 1930s–early 1940s. Lassiter himself noted in 1937 that "there is a growing demand for picnic areas for colored people. . . . Two bus loads are going up tomorrow."[35] And on August 17, 1939, the number of African American participants in a church picnic reached 385.[36]

In 1945, full desegregation was declared in all national parks. In 1947, Lewis Mountain and the dining room in Panorama at Swift Run Gap were integrated, and by 1950, the park was fully integrated, nearly ten years before all facilities in Virginia were forced to follow suit.

The drama of the Park's history with race relations is especially intriguing, when looking at Ickes's treatment of African American visitors to the Park. Since Ickes told Park Service employees not to point out the segregated areas to African American visitors, how did they know to go to Lewis Mountain, specifically?

One answer could be found in a remarkable primary source on African American tourism, "The Negro Motorist Green Book." First published in 1936 out of New York with assistance from the United States Travel Bureau, the yearly guide contained a list, by state, of restaurants, hotels, tourist cabins (including Lewis Mountain), bars, beauty salons, and service stations that catered to African Americans. "Correspondents," both white and African American, traveled to all areas of the United States to report on racial climates and availability of services through observation and interviews. Individuals who lived in specific areas also served as reporters who provided information on racial climates. One correspondent from North Dakota wrote:

We don't have any Negro families living in our city or community and consequently would have no occasion to offer housing, etc., to the Negro. I believe if Negro travelers were to pass thru Devil's Lake they would be treated as well as anyone else. The situation has never presented itself to this community to my knowledge, and therefore I am at a loss as to what they would encounter in this vicinity.[37]

Delving into the potential of these books as research sources for African American tourism is beyond the scope of this study, but combined with oral history research they could yield new and revealing perspectives on African American tourism and race relations in mid-century America.

Not all African American resorts were shrouded with controversy. By the early twentieth century, Black resorts began to dot the landscape, especially in northern locations, and even popular white resorts like Atlantic City, New Jersey, and Niagara Falls, New York had facilities for African Americans.[38] In Annapolis, Maryland, for example, Frederick Douglass's son, Lewis, built Highland Beach resort as a site to escape racism and enjoy the outdoors. This and other resorts, including southern beaches catered primarily to African Americans with the financial means and the necessary transportation to vacation. But many other Blacks, wishing to experience rest and relaxation tried to find other sites not so mainstream or elite, and much more vernacular in form.

During my fieldwork, I was fortunate enough to learn about one of these structures—African American tourist cabins in Luray, which housed African Americans in the 1950s (figure 12). I was even lucky enough to speak with Miss Martha Adams and tour the site. According to Miss Martha, individuals and families (most often six to ten people at a time) would show up at her door and ask if she had food and beds. She said, "I'd ask them how they heard of me and they said, well, we just asked in town and they told us to come and see you. I saw all kinds of people, white, black, and foreign."[39] Miss Martha described to me how visitors would sometimes simply picnic on her lawn; other overnight guests would "be up at night dancing and sometimes fighting."[40] The cabin I toured had a living room, a kitchen, and a small bedroom, and still contained its original furniture.

The location of Miss Martha's, at the margins of Luray, demonstrates a much different picture of tourism history, and one that has not been fully explored by tourism scholarship. Instead of being attracted to flashing lights from hotels and restaurants, African Americans were forced to find more private areas to stay in, if any at all, and to rely on the kindness of strangers who ran tourist cabins and homes. They could also depend on knowing the

Figure 12.   Black Inn

southern landscape and the layout of towns and cities to seek out the "Black" sections where they could find networks of boarding houses or, simply, hospitable homes. An African American man recalls traveling in the age of Jim Crow:

> When you live in the South and have been in the South all your life, you could find [places to eat and sleep] instinctively. Right now when I go into a strange county to hold court, I can go straight to the courthouse and [I] have never been there before. Southern towns are laid out in the same fashion, basically, and you could use your senses and sense where you are and where you're not. And if you keep driving, you can see the quality of the housing decreasing and blight setting in—abandoned cars and people hanging on the streets and then you can begin to see blacks. You know you're getting closer to the black community, and you can just go right in and find it. You may have to stop and ask someone: 'Where's the boarding house?' And you may be a block or two from it. It wasn't hard to find. You could find it instinctively.[41]

One of the most influential paradigms in tourism scholarship—that tourists seek authentic experiences to escape from their inauthentic everyday lives—disregards any diversity in the touristic experience. Sociologist Dean Mac-Cannell, the creator of this paradigm argues in his seminal, *The Tourist: A*

New Theory of the Leisure Class, that tourists set out on quests to find authenticity—an authentic lifestyle, authentic goods, authentic nature—and can never quite locate and experience it. When considering race, tourism, and the history of segregation in the south, the quest for authenticity and never finding it is meaningless when the concern was simply finding an actual place to eat and sleep. Moreover, touristic sites, he and other scholars assert, are only simulacra—vacuous spaces that sometimes exploit and commodify cultures and can never be genuine. In the case of African American tourist destinations, these sites were so few and far between for many Blacks, that the spaces were most likely seen as havens, not artificial places. More recently, Barbara Kirshenblatt-Gimblett has stated:

> Both heritage and tourism deal in the intangible, absent, inaccessible, fragmentary, and dislocated. These are features of the life world itself, which is one reason for the appeal and impossibility of the wholeness promised by the various worlds and lands of exhibitions, whether in museums or theme parks.[42]

This postmodern and ahistorical explanation of tourist sites does not adequately reflect what everyone has experienced as a tourist since historically, the tourist landscape was segregated. As with public history, new explorations, new definitions, and new methodologies need to be discovered and cultivated to seek out experiences of African Americans as tourists. I found Miss Martha only through an African American informant, not in any newspapers from the 1950s, proving that ethnography is one such way, maybe the best way, to find the more private spaces where history is made and stored.

Although the Shenandoah Battlefields Commission passed over Page County as a site for a visitor's center, tourism is a vital part of Luray's economy as it depends heavily on the Caverns and on the SNP, and has for almost the entire twentieth century. But after having spoken to several town officials and to citizens, it became clear that tourism, although wanted and needed, could be better managed and more fully exploited. The reasons for this lack of a coherent, efficient plan, according to my informants, range from ignorance on the part of the town council to poor planning, and in several occasions to a "good old boy" mentality, also described as a "good old boy" network. These responses came from informants who are considered transplants or outsiders, two of whom quit their jobs rather abruptly during my fieldwork.

Nearly all of my informants, when asked about tourism and any "impact" outsiders may have on the community and cultural identity, referred to the retirees from northern Virginia, Washington, DC, and other cities on the east coast who are arriving in substantial numbers. These newcomers, largely retirees, want to come in and change things. A town official told me:

> Most people don't object to tourism here. The tensions come from Page County society from the people who are newcomers who come from Northern Virginia and the stressed out life of the northeast corridor who come here and they initially come here and wow there's low property taxes, and this nice countryside and wouldn't it be nice to have a place here and let's go buy a mansion in Page County. Then they say why don't we have this facility in Page County. Are these people backward?[43]

This new group is also blamed for starting a "war" with the farmers over the issue of chicken litter and the foul odor it emits, a conflict that is centered on poultry farms, one of the most important industries in Luray (I=Interviewer):

> I think this has always been an agricultural community and that's the cornerstone of how Page County was built and growth is inevitable and so is change, and as the growth came out through the three towns, they tried to push this tourism atmosphere which was encroaching on the farmers and the tourists started to complain about the smell of chicken litter in the air that was spread after a chicken house had been cleaned out. And that's how it started. Luray passed a law that said that you cannot haul chicken litter through the town. And it sort of became anti-farming and that's just occurred recently within the past 5–10 years, this anti-farming sentiment.

> *I*: And that's from the tourists?

> That's from the tourists and some of the residents who have moved here who have never lived here initially, retirees who have come here to spend their retirement years. We get a lot of them from the federal government, CIA, FBI, and other agencies. And so the farmers banded together and said look, this has been a farming community and always will be one and that's how the war started.[44]

This war between insiders and outsiders is not just a conflict based on the right to haul chicken litter through the streets and curb the smell; the attack on the poultry houses is a direct attack on Luray's agricultural way of life, at the core of their culture. Due to the poultry smell controversy, and other complaints received from these newcomers, the Board of Supervisors adopted a resolution in the summer of 1999 that Page County was, above all else, an agricultural county. Part of the resolution reads:

> Owners, occupants, and users of land in the agriculture district should be prepared to accept such inconveniences or discomfort as a normal and necessary aspect of living in a zoning district in a county with a strong rural character and

an active agricultural sector. As agricultural land is a primary resource and economic asset of the county, it must be preserved to the greatest extent possible.[45]

This backlash against change is a pronouncement for sustaining cultural identity in the midst of change not just from outsiders, but from the possibilities of sprawl the outsiders might bring with them. An informant told me:

> The problem we "locals" [quotations hers] have with some outsiders is that some come here because the tax base is so low, yet they want big-city amenities, that would require higher taxes to support. And sometimes there is a superior attitude toward us "mountain people." [quotation hers] Some want to change everything and become impatient because THEY WANT WHAT THEY WANT AND THEY WANT [IT] RIGHT NOW! [capitalization hers].[46]

This informant, though, also insisted to me that outsiders are actually being accepted; that times are changing. She believes that acceptance lies in "their willingness to volunteer for charitable organizations."[47] Another informant told me that, however, "overnight changes will find resistance on all sides."[48]

In addition to influencing and being influenced by the tourism trade, Luray remains an idealistic small town, where most residents feel safe from crime. It has suffered from the decline of large-scale manufacturing plants, which dominated the economy during the mid-1900s, leaving many residents who want to work in occupations outside of the service industries commuting to Washington, DC and other locations in more eastern and northern areas of Virginia to find higher paying jobs.

Provocatively, the interests of the locals, the transplants, the tourists to Luray and officials in the Shenandoah National Park are also met by a common resolution and efforts toward fending off sprawl and development. A town official described to me how

> . . . tourism and agriculture now are linked. And it's not just because we have tourist-related activities on the farm, but it is, I talked to the National Park Superintendent up here and I asked him about how he would like to see Page County developed. The rural viewscapes are a great tourist attraction. He said if Northern Virginia was sprawled out down in the Valley, there wouldn't be near the tourist increases . . . so there we have the meeting of the two: we have tourism both from the local tourist industry and from the Park, tourists demanding or desiring rural landscapes to be preserved. The farmer also wants to preserve their agricultural lands and if they manage to do that then the rural landscape will be preserved.[49]

In the end, both parties in the traditional tourist relationship, host and guest, want the same thing—to preserve the agricultural landscape, albeit for different

reasons. It is the third party, the "postmodern" tourists, who are complicating
the equation, even though they too do not want to see and live with sprawl from
which they fled. Since this literal common ground has already been found, perhaps finding a solution to the influx of retirees will be foreseeable in the future,
and the preservation of the landscape will continue to be the first priority.

The tourist experience often begins in Luray, as in many other destination
spots, with a guidebook, map, or brochure, literary staples in visitors' centers
around the world. Describing "key" and "important" sites to visit within a
given area, this literature plays a central role in determining where a tourist
goes, but also what is worthy of seeing. Since these sources comprise what is
essential to know about a place and how to experience a place and its history,
they are embedded in the touristic experience, but also in power dynamics
and ideology. What I discovered is that in the touristic literature, historical
narratives, and the commemorative landscape, the same stories of the first
families, the Civil War, and the Confederacy receive attention and endorse-
ment as they have for many years. The seemingly innocuous tourism literature, then, is an ideological tool, contributing to a biased view of history and
public history. Further, maps, guidebooks, and brochures, like historical narratives and public history sites, are political tools, embracing and containing
only the history and places that are considered important. Casteneda believes
maps are "models of totalized and totalizing knowledge," and "correspond to
strategies of power and places."[50] Touristic literature prioritizes the landscape
and history, and the tourist's experience of them.

Tourism literature also does not provide details about a site's history with
tourism; in Luray's case, it does not describe how the community has resisted and negotiated power with outside groups, and preserved its agricultural and commemorative landscapes. It also does not discuss how the SNP
battled with integration, and how African Americans found places to stay not
from flashing lights on the highway, but through Green Books and word of
mouth. Instead, for the most part, tourist books and tours continue to expose
tourists to predictable, one-dimensional history, and an uncritical understanding of the complexity of the public history around them.

The tourism experience is not, however, simply a superficial one, as some
tourism scholars, including Dean MacCannell have suggested. As we have
seen, interpretation designed to attract tourists (interpretation of the Civil War)
is serious business in Luray and the Shenandoah Valley, even though it lacks,
I argue, a comprehensive picture of life in the Valley, especially in terms of an
African American experience. Interpretive messages designed for tourists are
also crucial to the nearby National Park Service at SNP, which recently took
down a show that it and local citizens (some from Luray) felt exhibited bad
history to the millions of visitors who have traveled through the Park in the last
sixty years. The old show, which lasted for nearly forty years, told a biased and

inaccurate story of the mountain people who were displaced to create the SNP. A citizen's group that includes Luray citizens and the Park Service, showing that the history tourists are exposed to does matter, rebuilt a remarkable and even risky show, offering tourists something new—a politicized perspective on history, and not just a rehashing of great people and great events. In the next chapter I look at both of these exhibitions, and discuss how this new show offers not only fresh perspectives on how history is exhibited, but also the potential for exhibitions to challenge tourists to think critically about history.

NOTES

1. Susan Braselton Fant, Preservation Partners, LLC, "Interpretation Summary Sheet," Shenandoah Valley Battlefields National Historic District Commission. Received December 1999, property of author.

2. Quetzil Castaneda, *In the Museum of Maya Culture: Touring Chichen Itza* (Minneapolis: University of Minnesota Press, 1996), 7.

3. Casteneda, *In the Museum of Maya Culture*, 9.

4. Erve Chambers, ed. *Tourism and Culture: An Applied Perspective* (Albany: State University of New York, 1997), 7.

5. "A Peek Inside: A Look at the Valley's Caverns," *Page News & Courier*, 20–21 September 2000, Valley Overlook Section.

6. "Luray Caverns Backgrounder" printed by Luray Caverns Corporation, Luray, Virginia, n/d.

7. Barbara G. Carson, "Early American Tourists and the Commercialization of Leisure" in Cary Carson, Ronald Hoffman, and Peter J. Albert in *Of Consuming Interests: The Style of Life in the Eighteenth Century* (Charlottesville, 1994), 373–405.

8. Barbara Babcock Lassiter, *American Wilderness: The Hudson River School of Painting* (Garden City, NY, 1978), x.

9. William Cronon, "The Trouble With Wilderness," in *The Best American Essays 1996*, Geoffrey C. Ward, ed. (New York: Houghton Mifflin, 1996), 83–109.

10. Gurnee, *Discovery of Luray Caverns*, 53.

11. Gurnee, *Discovery of Luray Caverns*, 55. There is no date listed for this report, although it was probably written in the 1880s.

12. Dona Brown, *Inventing New England: Regional Tourism in the Nineteenth Century* (Washington, DC: Smithsonian Institution Press, 1995), 117.

13. See Jane Stewart Becker, "Selling Tradition: The Domestication of Southern Appalachian Culture in 1930s America." Ph.D. diss., Boston University, 1993.

14. Elizabeth Ann Atwood, "'Saratoga of the South': Tourism in Luray, Virginia, 1878–1905" Master's Thesis, University of Virginia, Corcoran Dept. of History, May 1983, p. 19.

15. *The Page Courier*, 24 August 1882.

16. Atwood, "Saratoga of the South," 21, 22.

17. Atwood, "Saratoga of the South," 25.

18. Atwood, "Saratoga of the South," 26.

19. Atwood, "Saratoga of the South," 35.

20. Atwood, "Saratoga of the South," 29.

21. Atwood, "Saratoga of the South," epilogue.

22. *Page News & Courier*, 11 January 2001.

23. Charlie Thomas. Interview by the author. August 1999.

24. Howard J. Kittell, Executive Director of Commission, personal correspondence, 17 May 1999.

25. Kittell correspondence.

26. "Shenandoah Valley Battlefields National Historic District Commission Summary Report of 30-day Public Comment Period for Phase Two of the Action Plan: Developing Options and Strategies," Susan Braselton Fant, Preservation Partners, LLC, November 1999.

27. Pollack, *Skyland,* 46.

28. Pollack, *Skyland*, 22.

29. Pollack, *Skyland*, 22.

30. Pollack, *Skyland,* 187.

31. Engle, Reed L. "Shenandoah: Laboratory for Change," *CRM: Cultural Resource Management: Shenandoah: Managing Cultural Resources in a Natural Park"* 21 (1998): 34–35.

32. Lambert, *The Undying Past,* 259.

33. Lambert, *The Undying Past*, 260.

34. Engle, "Shenandoah: Laboratory," 35.

35. Engle, "Shenandoah: Laboratory," 35.

36. Lambert, *The Undying Past,* 259.

37. "The Negro Motorist Green Book" (New York: Victor H. Green & Co., 1948), 3–4.

38. Cindy S. Aron, *Working At Play: A History of Vacations in the United States* (New York, Oxford University Press, 1999), 214.

39. Miss Martha Adams. Interview by the author. January 2000.

40. Adams Interview, January 2000.

41. William H. Chafe, ed. *Remembering Jim Crow: African Americans Tell About Life in the Segregated South* (New York: The New Press, 2001), 131.

42. Barbara Kirshenblatt-Gimblett, *Destination Culture: Tourism, Museums, and Heritage* (Berkeley: University of California Press, 1998), 167.

43. Carl Butler. Interview by the author. 26 July 1999.

44. Jack Sutter. Interview by the author. 18 February 1999.

45. Resolution, Board of Supervisors, County of Page, Virginia, "Notice of Agricultural Operations" 9 July 1999. Located in Clerk's Office, Circuit Court, Luray, Virginia.

46. Felicia Monroe. E-mail to the author. 25 July 2000.

47. Monroe Email, 25 July 2000.

48. John Waybright. E-mail to the author. 21 November 2006.

49. Carl Butler. Interview by the author. 26 July 1999.

50. Casteneda, Museum of Maya Culture, 3.

Chapter Five

Recapturing Identity:
The "Life on the Mountain" Exhibition
at Shenandoah National Park

If Luray's citizens were able to assert and sustain their own conceptions of heritage throughout the last century, one important public history arena existed over which they and members of neighboring counties had no control—an exhibition in the Shenandoah National Park's visitor's center. Mounted in 1966 during the National Park Service's "Mission 66" initiative to improve services and interpretation for visitors, the show portrayed the people to fit a particular ideology: that the removal of the native mountain culture was justified to "construct" a national park.

In this chapter I explore and deconstruct this controversial first exhibition and the new, more historically accurate show installed in 2000. I argue that for a period of over one hundred years, missionaries, educators, social scientists, and the National Park Service (NPS) constructed a specific cultural identity of the mountain people. These outside groups relied on cultural stereotypes of an impoverished, yet folk, community, devoted to hard, manual labor and craftmaking, to satisfy their various agendas. Recent research performed by archaeologists, historians, local citizens and even NPS employees suggests, however, that the mountain people were relatively sophisticated consumers, socioculturally and racially diverse, vital workers involved in the turn-of-the-century tourism trade and the SNP, and actively negotiated the turmoil of resettlement.

The exhibition space, while approximately forty-five minutes by car from Luray, is, nonetheless, vital to a study of the public history of Luray. Citizens and tourist groups from Luray were involved in the planning stages of the Park in the 1920s; most Luray natives and businesses welcomed the potential tourism dollars.[1]

The exhibition site is also important to this study because it is one of the only public history sites devoted to the culture, people, and history of this area. Travelers passing through the Park get their only exposure to those who live in the Valley through this exhibition. Unfortunately, for nearly forty years, not only did the first exhibition paint a one-dimensional and tendentious story of the people who lived in the mountains, it failed and the new exhibition still fails to differentiate between the mountain people and the inhabitants in Luray, and excludes African American history, problems acknowledged by Park Service employees.[2]

Fortunately, a local community organization, The Children of the Shenandoah (COS), along with better-trained and more sensitive historians at the National Park Service in the SNP, constructed a more equitable portrait of the mountain people and the story of the Park, proving that revising exhibitions and recapturing heritage may be challenging, but it is also feasible. This is an idea many academics and historians suggest, but to which they rarely offer actual solutions.

What the new exhibition does do, however, is set an example for creating an engaging and critical public history display: it reveals the potential for local communities to be involved in the public interpretation of their history. Through oral histories, remarkable and even shocking photos, and comprehensive text panels, including one which discusses the formation of stereotypes, the exhibition reveals the many motivations of the Park planners and sacrifices of the local inhabitants of both the Valley and the mountains who helped to create this Park. From visitor feedback received thus far, the exhibition is receiving promising reviews ranging from "It doesn't tell you what to think," and "We never would have come here had we known what really happened."[3]

Dedicated in 1936 by Franklin Roosevelt, the Shenandoah National Park was built during the Great Depression to provide men with jobs and to serve as a source of repose for urbanites suffering from the economic and emotional ills of this period. The idea of an eastern national park had been a topic of discussion since the 1920s, when Herbert Hoover created a trout-fishing camp near what is now the Big Meadows visitor's center located on the northern end of the park. Park enthusiasts gained support from local citizens, including those living in Luray, and businesses were eager for the financial and economic gains from the tourists. But the problem with establishing a park lay in the fact that the land had to be donated to the national government and purchased by the state of Virginia. The other significant obstacle was the "problem" of the nearly 450 families who lived within the Park's boundaries. After many debates, the mountain people were relocated in resettlement communities in the Valley, including one in Luray. Although some individuals and families were actually happy to leave the mountains, some who wanted to stay took their cases to the Supreme Court.[4]

Park and government officials discussed the idea of keeping the residents in the Park to entertain the tourists, but Roosevelt ultimately decided that the people would need to be removed so that the land could return to its "original" state, yielding an empty park that would be better suited to promote the "material and psychological well being" of American citizens.[5] The rejuvenation rhetoric of Roosevelt's dedication speech neatly illustrates the NPS's goals, for he claimed that SNP would provide an emotional escape for the visitors who battle with the "rush and strain" of urban life.

The NPS did not create an exhibition at SNP until the mid-1960s, the time of the "Mission 66" initiative, a national effort aimed at improving visitor services and interpretation in the National Park system. According to historian John Bodnar, this new drive to satisfy patrons grew out of a desire to further promote the NPS's founding ideas, ideologies, and values, but was also a response to the urban unrest of the 1960s. As national parks served as sites which provided repose for the social ills and potential unrest of the 1930s, the Park Service also responded to threats to the national order in its individual parks in the turbulent 1960s. Bodnar writes:

> . . . the NPS discovered that its basic devotion to patriotism and national unity that had served it well in the past could be readily adopted to new needs generated by a society becoming conscious of dealing with political problems in its growing urban areas. . . . In the thirties the NPS found that symbols of patriotism and unity were viewed as crucial by national leaders who determined its budget and who wished to lessen the appeal of any ideology that appeared to threaten national unity. In the 1960s urban populations, especially disaffected minorities, posed a threat to national unity and civic order, and the NPS recognized again that it must direct its symbolic messages in strategic directions.[6]

The messages of the exhibition constructed in the 1960s were ideological, promoting the idea that the removal of the people for the Park was necessary and inevitable, and that nature is inherently restorative and culture essentially destructive. Thus, nature and culture were bifurcated, with nature being the most important and durable agent in the equation. This one-dimensional and selective exhibition also told a linear, progressive history starting from the first Americans to the return of nature for the Park, and was designed "to show just how far the nation had moved civilization beyond the level of the Native Americans."[7]

This exhibition, installed in 1966, lacked dates and emphasized the park's establishment. It took the visitor on a "progress of civilization" journey that followed this track: presence of Native Americans, settlement of Anglo-Europeans, establishment of self-sufficient farms, and finally the return of the wilderness. The three distinct cultures were poorly represented. Their ways of life appeared static, and the mountain people were thrown back into a time in the 1930s, although this decade was not stated until near the end. They experienced their demise with the passing of time, the chestnut blight that struck the area in the 1920s, and the advancement of civilization. Nature, on the other hand, was alive, full of wildlife and constantly changing, busy returning to its "primordial" state.

The visitor was first confronted with a wall of six panels stretching about thirty feet and encompassing some 10,000 years of history. The visitor saw arrowheads, eighteenth century surveying equipment and maps, but most intriguing were the last four panels that textually and visually represented the mountain people at the time of the Park's establishment. The section began with a diorama of a mountain home labeled, "A Mountain Homestead," consisting of a doll-house sized version of a "typical" home equipped with figures of men chopping wood and a woman standing on the porch. The most striking part of this display was the lack of a date. This panel immediately follows the one illustrating the surveying of the land in the Valley in the 1700s. Since the exhibition is arranged chronologically, a visitor may assume that this homestead resembles one from the eighteenth or nineteenth century. The absence of a date, and the implication that this homestead is "typical" (there were no others displayed), showed that the Park Service viewed the culture as homogeneous and stuck in time.

This display failed to acknowledge the socioeconomic and racial diversity in this area of the Blue Ridge Mountains: throughout the nineteenth and twentieth centuries, homes ranged from one-room cabins, which were the only housing forms represented in the old show, to large plantations. John West, an African American, owned 812 acres in Augusta County, one of the counties affected by the park's establishment, and located about fifty miles from Page County.[8]

The three panels that followed the diorama were entitled, "How Man Used the Mountain." Displayed were artifacts related to farm labor with text describing the efficiency of the men and the instruments they used: axes and other tools related to the timber industry, an apple peeler, and cherry pitter. The most provocative element in this display was the title. By choosing the word "used," the Park Service relied on a rhetoric of exploitation when describing the mountain peoples' lifestyles. No mention is made of the timber industries that primarily contributed to the denuding of the mountains that were to become the park. Historian Darwin Lambert notes, "But nearly all the large timber tracts were owned by people who lived outside the park-land, though most of them within a mile or two, like the farmer-grazers."[9]

The next section centered on what was assumed to be typical "women's" work and the tools of production this entailed. A loom, two spinning wheels, a small rug with a photograph of its creator and a series of three small panels described how wool was spun. Women, the exhibition asserted, were responsible only for spinning wool and making rugs, and that they were the only clothes- and craftmakers consigned to domestic work. Yet this gender bifurcation is grossly inaccurate, as women contributed substantially to the economic survival of the mountain home. Women grew and canned vegetables, chopped wood, and performed other physically-intensive tasks outside of the home.[10] Men, as well, blurred the public and private spheres by making crafts, including weaving baskets, a longstanding Blue Ridge folk craft.

All of the objects selected to represent the mountain men signified agrarian labor. The message these artifacts conveyed said that mountain men were, first and foremost, producers, devoted to economic prosperity the old-fashioned way, through honest hard work. This emphasis on production suggests that the mountain men were prosperous agrarians, upstanding capitalists, and creative toolmakers, but it also masks the other social forces that existed in the Shenandoah Valley, and proves that the image of the mountain culture is a construction of modern, industrialized society. Mark Leone's comments on the representation of Shakers at Shakertown, an outdoor living history museum, rang frighteningly true for the representation of Shenandoah Valley dwellers: "To see Shaker industry as efficient, profitable, logical and ingenious is to see it with accuracy devoid of analysis. It is to see culture as rising from function, behavior from efficiency, and thought from material necessity."[11] To see the mountain people solely as creative producers is to throw their culture into a romanticized, pioneer past. Americans still maintain a tight grip on agrarian idealism and the wholesome virtues of a rural lifestyle. But no panels existed to reveal that both men and women worked beyond their farms. As we have seen, women and men worked in the tourism industry in the early twentieth century by working for George Freeman Pollock's resort, Skyland, and later for the NPS. Former Blue Ridge resident Richard Beaty sold one of Darwin Lambert's guidebooks during the same time period outside one of the park's entrances.[12]

This crafted image of Blue Ridge mountain people is not only contained and dispersed throughout the Shenandoah Valley, it pervades the entire Southern Appalachian region. In "The Blue Ridge Parkway and the Myths of the

Pioneer," Phil Noblitt deconstructs the carefully staged creation of a pioneer culture displayed to visitors who traverse the Blue Ridge Parkway. He describes how the Park Service manipulated sites to make them look more bucolic and pre-industrial:

> In designing and developing the Parkway, landscape architects and park managers consciously strived to portray the Blue Ridge region as a land of isolated and independent pioneers. They not only built miles of split-rail fences and selectively retained and reconstructed log cabins and farmsteads, but they also systematically removed or excluded from view elements that did not fit. For example, not a single clapboard farmhouse was preserved within the boundaries of the Parkway, even though such houses were common in the region by the latter half of the 19th century. Visible signs of industrialization were also eliminated or screened.[13]

By removing industrialization, the Park Service aimed to create a pre-modern, authentic past. The people of the Parkway, as in the Shenandoah Valley, were heaped together, thrown back into an idealized, pioneer past, and displayed. Mountain people as agents of change, as social actors engaged in dense webs of social relations, and as individuals capable of adapting to and accepting technological change were buried under the reconstructed log cabins in the exhibition.

The last panel on the mountain people is a large photograph of a mountain man sitting on his wooden porch, staring out into the landscape. The caption read:

> With the chestnut gone and woods quickly denuded of other commercial timber, the mountain man faced a bleak future. The land, degraded by years of fire, poor farming methods and erosion was no longer fruitful. Hope lay in the world beyond the coves, but he was ill-prepared and unwilling to leave his mountain home.

The black and white photograph and the prose created a melodramatic display implying that the mountain people were to blame for their fate after they left the mountains. The description "ill-prepared" constructed an image of a people who knew removal was coming but just did not properly prepare themselves for it. As it turns out, however, most mountain people adjusted to their Resettlement Administration homesteads and new homes in the foothills of the mountains. This panel is particularly significant because it is the one that most offends citizens who now belong to the COS. This panel will be further discussed in the next section.

By making spurious generalizations about the mountain people, the Park Service overlooked their ability to negotiate their resettlement. Not all the mountain people were "unwilling" to leave their homes: some wanted to re-settle in more inhabited areas to take advantage of educational and professional opportunities in the Valley and elsewhere. When Virgil Corbin was relocated in 1937, he was employed by the National Youth Administration—a New Deal agency—to make crafts for $16.00 per month. He claims that leaving the mountain and working for the NYA in Luray, Virginia was a "good experience" and that he "wouldn't want to go back" to his mountain home.[14] Instead of discussing how the people actually did negotiate and renegotiate their social location, the display was meant to evoke sympathy for the "plight" of these impoverished (which is their fault), uncivilized, and stubborn people.

The final section of the exhibition celebrated the establishment of the park and the diversity of wildlife that the park contains. Exhibited were several photographs of Civilian Conservation Corps men digging and erecting road walls, the silver shovel used at the groundbreaking of the park, and a series of panels on animals. The visitor left the exhibition knowing that the only inhabitants of the park are owls, bear, deer, bobcats, and other creatures.

This section also demonstrated the theme of nature's dynamism, its ability to withstand change and exploitation, and the hope that untouched nature would provide peaceful repose for a nation plagued by unemployment and despair. Nature was reconstructed as a pristine haven for the urban middle class and still is. In the old exhibition, nature is "museumized"—removed from its actual evolution and its relationship to culture, and placed inside an interpretive bubble, apart from the harmful effects from humanity. The separation of nature and culture signified that the people in the area were simply not as important as the preservation of nature and the marking-off of the land as a vacation area for the middle class.

While the social construction of nature, especially in the making of national parks, is rejected in favor of a deterministic history in the previous exhibition, it is a key theme in the revised show as well as in some of the SNP's new interpretive programs. According to a Park Service employee, these new efforts, included in Boy Scout and adult programs, are being well received in the community.[15]

Crucial absences from the old exhibition and from historical narratives of the mountain people were their trends of consumption. Carolyn and Jack Reeder, cultural historians of the Blue Ridge Mountains, first suggested the possibility that the mountain people were not as impoverished as history and popular texts and myths would have us believe. In looking at old home sites, they found items such as stoves, sewing machines, and decorative glassware and china.[16] And currently, important archeological digs have been undertaken in separate hollows in the Blue Ridge that reveal that the mountain people

were active consumers, not simply craft makers with no ties to the industrialized world. A recent on-line report on these digs states that:

> Yet the recently-examined material record indicates that even in Corbin Hollow
> [considered the most impoverished area of the Blue Ridge], popular descriptions
> of mountain isolation and degeneracy were overblown. Typical assemblages
> range from decorative tablewares, pharmaceutical bottles and automobile parts
> to mail-order toys, furniture, shoes, and even fragments of 78 rpm records.[17]

One noteworthy discovery occurred in Nicholson Hollow where a house ruin
is possibly a slave quarter from the 1820s, showing that mountain people
were not all self-sufficient and utilized slave labor.[18]

Tourists and citizens alike, according to Park Service employees, were actively criticizing the impoverished image of the mountain people in the
1980s. The first complaints centered on the gendered language of the title of
the exhibition, "Man on the Mountain," and the gender stereotypes advertised
in the show. In the early 1990s, the COS, comprising both descendents of the
displaced mountain families and other citizens, formed and made changing
the exhibition their first priority.[19] Well aware that millions of visitors were
viewing the inaccurate and biased show, they felt that changing the show
would have an important and ubiquitous impact. Concomitantly, SNP gained
a cultural historian and an interpretive staff well-trained and sensitive to the
requests of COS.

One of the biggest complaints of the old show, according to a COS member, was the picture of a mountain man looking out over a mountain vista with
the caption, "it was time to move on," implying the people could not adjust
to life in the lowlands. That the mountain people did not know how to survive
or culturally adapt was one of the most offensive messages of the old exhibition. The new show helps to rectify this myth through panels of transcribed
oral histories that detail how some mountain residents appreciated the new
opportunities of life in the Valley.

Upon entering the "Life on the Mountain" show, which is mounted in the
same straight hallway as the previous show, the visitor finds the right side devoted to the economic and social life of the mountain people, and the left side
a series of vertical panels chronologically covering what was occurring
worldwide and in the Park's planning history, beginning in 1926. Unlike the
old exhibition, this show immediately sets dates and places the Park's story
in a cultural context.

The first section of the exhibition on the right side describes the work of
Miriam Sizer, an educator and social worker who, after her work in five
mountain hollows, was responsible for perpetuating negative stereotypes of
the mountain people by claiming the people were destitute and in need of ed-

ucation. Sizer, as the panel notes, was not the only individual to create and spread biased perceptions of the mountain people. In 1933, social workers Mandel Sherman and Thomas R. Henry traveled to some of the hollows and printed an egregiously slanted work, *Hollow Folk*, a much detested book with many citizens even today.[20] According to their book, the hollows were a study of "the growth and decline of human culture."[21]

The next section concentrates on the diversity of economic conditions of the mountain dwellers through primary source materials. Documents itemizing the amount of the estates of several families are on view, revealing, for example, that where Charlie Nicholson's property was worth a little over $50, John Alexander and his family's land was valued at over $56,000. Photographs of the properties, ranging from a modest cabin to a two-story house, also attest to the range of socioeconomic conditions of the mountain culture.

Concomitantly, on the left side of the show, the story of the displacement of the people in the early 1930s begins to unfold and culminates with a revealing and even shocking photograph of a mountain resident being forcibly removed by government officials from his property. When I first viewed this photo, I was quite surprised that the Park Service would mount it, given the picture it paints of the national government. When I asked a Park Service employee about this issue, she felt that displaying the photo was no big deal because, "It's the truth. It's kind of like the Holocaust Museum which makes a lot of people look bad but that's what happened and that's the way of the world."[22]

The final section of the exhibition is a floor-to-ceiling collage of faces of the mountain people interspersed with quotations ranging from acrimonious comments about the Park to acknowledgements that leaving the mountains was not so bad after all. Thus, visitors leave this short but poignant show with pictures of people who made it possible for all the visitors to visit and enjoy this land as a national park. In this new show, nature takes a back seat to the cultural history of the mountains, and is seen not as needing to return to a constructed primordial state, but as a recreational space for which great human sacrifice was made. Nature and culture, at first diametrically opposed in the old show, are now intertwined, and a much more balanced and accurate story of the Park's establishment is exhibited.

For all of its novel perspectives and interpretations, the exhibition does not, however, interpret two critical subjects: first, it does not mention the presence of African Americans either in the mountains or in the Valley, and it does not differentiate between the people living in the mountains and in the Valley, including the residents of Luray. Visitors will still neither learn about racial diversity nor diversity within the white communities. Fortunately, however, SNP employees are trying to obtain funds to explore African American history in this region, showing they are concerned about their absence in the exhibition.[23]

That the Park Service was willing to listen to the COS and make an exhibition change is a sign that a local community has a voice in how its culture and its perceptions of the history of its culture are represented to tourists. The quest for a new show also proves that tourism and interpretation at tourist sites should be taken seriously. Unlike some tourism scholars, including Mac-Cannell and Daniel Boorstin, who argue that the touristic experience is inescapably "inauthentic" and specious, the COS and Park Service do not see tourism in the same light: if they did, they would not have been so concerned with the interpretive messages of the previous exhibition. The revision of the show reveals that tourists constitute an audience whose judgments matter and who are capable of understanding the complexities of history, not just facts about great events and great people. Perhaps most importantly, visitors are entering into a dialogue about the history with which they are presented and not simply asked to accept the grandeur of the natural world—they are learning about the human *and* environmental costs involved in creating parks in the NPS. As Mark Leone writes in his examination of Carter's Grove, a historical area of Colonial Williamsburg, ". . . why not offer a critique of the United States instead of only teaching mainstream history?"[24] The new exhibition does just this: it offers a critical, informed, and even risky view of a darker moment in history as it tries to heal battle wounds between the Park Service and the local community. Public history has the power to falsify and simplify history, but it also has the power, especially when local communities are involved, to resuscitate it and give it new life.

Academics such as Richard Handler, Michael Wallace, and Michael Shanks and Christopher Tilley have all criticized public history sites, including living history villages like Colonial Williamsburg, or entertainment parks such as Walt Disney World and Epcot Center. Wallace, for example, vilifies the corporate history displayed at Disney and Epcot, and its ideological message of how technological progress has "naturally" evolved.[25] While insightful and theoretically sophisticated, these studies are often devoid of solutions for rectifying public history sites. Shanks and Tilley, however, do offer suggestions toward "redeeming" museum displays, and some of their suggestions are contained in the new exhibition. For example, they state, "The museum can allow the visitor to construct a past along with the archaeologist-curator: participation not as a means to a pre-given, pre-discovered end, but as an open process of constructing different pasts."[26] In "Interpreting History Through Objects," Barbara Carson outlines a methodology for improving interpretation emphasizing the idea that ". . . goods are imbedded in social process."[27] This perspective, she argues, emphasizes the dynamic, changing relationships humans have with material objects.

In the old show, the inevitable historical end of the story of the SNP was its returning to an untouched nature; all human action and interaction needed to be stopped for this to occur. But the new show answers Shanks's and Tilley's as well as Carson's request: The different perspectives, motivations, and emotions of the mountain communities, the NPS, and citizens' groups are offered for the visitors. Maybe, most importantly to Shanks and Tilley, is to "introduce political content into conventional displays—show how the past may be manipulated and misrepresented for present purposes."[28] Indeed, the new exhibition's principal thematic current is very political since it centers on how and why cultural stereotypes and nature itself were displayed and interpreted to suit the ends of the NPS.

In researching this exhibition and in seeking out informants and in interviews, I realized that tension exists between COS and the Park Service, even though the exhibition is being well-accepted among tourists and locals alike. But this tension is not illustrated in the exhibition—visitors cannot tell that mistrust and suspicion lie beneath the planning and construction of this show. Park Service employees are vague about how much credit the COS should have for the revamping of the show, and are willing to give them credit if this satisfies them. The COS seems to be uncertain as to how much of an effect it actually did have on the exhibition.

The strained relationship between the Park Service, the COS, and other members of the community was exacerbated four years ago by the Park Service's decision to close the Park's archives for the construction of a new facility. A local citizen who wanted to research his family (one that had been relocated in the 1930s) was denied access and a battle ensued. According to an article that made it into *The Washington Post*, the citizen was concerned that the Park Service was leaving the archives closed so it could go through files and selectively remove any self-deprecating information on the Park's origins. The Park denied these allegations, arguing that the building had to remain closed to catalogue artifacts, documents, and photographs more professionally.[29] Previously, the records, photographs, and even reel-to-reel tapes of rich historical data were stored in a house-like structure, without professional museum storage and environmental standards. Having been in the building, and knowing the limited budget of the Park Service at this time, I knew, firsthand, that the construction of a new complex was long overdue.

But the non-access led to locals complaining that this was another attempt by the NPS to deny the people something that is rightfully theirs—access to their families' records and artifacts who already had been wronged by the Park Service. But the archives opened again in Spring 2001, and an expansive website on SNP, including many historic digital images, is helping open up the past of the park to the world.

In many ways, though, the tensions that exist between the local communities and the NPS brought the new exhibition to fruition and will, perhaps, have the potential to settle interpretive and other issues in the future. What the revision of the show also reveals is that people should and want to have a direct effect on how their history is interpreted to the public. As the citizens of Luray have shown, marginalized rural communities affected by numbers of outsiders are anything but passive consumers and members of an exploited community. As I stated in chapter four, heritage celebrations in Luray began as the tourism industry burgeoned, revealing the importance of local expressions of heritage even when the scores of outsiders began to transform the town. Many Luray and mountain residents alike accepted the changes tourism sparked, resisted potentially culturally destructive corporate and economic forces that can accompany tourism, and profited from the trade. As well, like the slave auction block, which is also ensconced in controversy, the new exhibition proves how far individuals are willing to go to recapture heritage and to assert their presence in the historical record.

NOTES

1. Christine Cooper. Interview by the author. 28 December 2000.
2. Karla Michaels. Interview by the author. 28 December 2000.
3. Karla Michaels. Interview, 28 December 2000.
4. For a comprehensive overview of the displacement and resettlement of the mountain people, see Darwin Lambert, *The Undying Past of Shenandoah National Park* (Boulder: Roberts Rinehart, 1989); and a special supplement to the *Madison Eagle*, "Blue Ridge Exodus," 14 April 1996.
5. John Bodnar, *Remaking America: Public Memory, Commemoration, and Patriotism in the Twentieth Century* (Princeton: Princeton University Press, 1992), 178.
6. Bodnar, *Remaking America*, 197–98.
7. Bodnar, *Remaking America,* 181.
8. Lambert, *The Undying Past*, 178.
9. Lambert, *The Undying Past*, 160.
10. Lambert, *The Undying Past*, 165.
11. Mark Leone, "The Relationship Between Artifacts and the Public in Outdoor History Museums," in *Annals of the New York Academy of Sciences*, 305.
12. Lambert, *The Undying Past*, 177.
13. Phil Noblitt, "The Blue Ridge Parkway and Myths of the Pioneer," *Appalachian Journal*, 394.
14. Virgil Corbin. Interview with Dorothy Noble Smith, 1979. Tape recording, Shenandoah National Park Archives, Luray, Virginia.
15. Karla Michaels. Interview by the author. 28 December 2000.

16. Carolyn and Jack Reeder, *Shenandoah Vestiges: What the Mountain People Left Behind* (Vienna, Virginia: The Potomac Appalachian Trail Club, 1980) 34–36.

17. "Survey of Rural Mountain Settlement," http://www.history.org/cwf/argy/argyshen.htm page 3, 22 April 2000.

18. "Survey of Rural Mountain Settlement," 2.

19. Charlotte Hanson. Interview by the author. October 2000.

20. Lambert, *The Undying Past,* 185.

21. Lambert, *The Undying Past*, 185.

22. Christine Cooper. Interview by the author. 28 December 2000.

23. Karla Michaels. Interview by the author. 28 December 2000.

24. Mark Leone, Exhibition Review, *Journal of American History*, December 1992, 1082–87.

25. Michael Wallace, *Mickey Mouse History and Other Essays on American Memory* (Philadelphia: Temple University Press, 1996).

26. Michael Shanks and Christopher Tilley, *Presenting the Past: Re-Constructing Archaeology* (New York: Routledge, 1992), 98.

27. Barbara Carson, "Interpreting History Through Objects," *Journal of Museum Education* (10/3, Summer 1985), 129–33.

28. Carson, "Interpreting History," 129–33.

29. "Anger in Appalachia," *The Washington Post*, 6 March 2000.

Epilogue—Interpreting for the Future

"It feels good to reopen the past for future generations so possibly everyone can treat everyone equal and not be prejudiced."

Luray seventh grader on performing oral histories
with African American citizens

In July 2001, my informant, Frank, mailed me a small booklet put together by local seventh graders, "West Luray Remembered," a compilation of oral histories from some of Luray's senior African Americans. The students, according to Frank, sought to gain information on how Luray's African American citizens lived with and overcame segregation. Most of the informants recalled not being allowed to enter the front doors of restaurants, and having to sit in the balcony of the theatre on Main Street, throwing popcorn on the white people seated below. This booklet yielded positive responses from both the students and informants, with similar projects slated to begin September 2001.

The booklet a valuable piece of ethnographic work—reveals the importance of recording voices and experiences never heard, a central goal of this dissertation, and showed the students a part of Luray's history they had not known about before. The de facto segregation that exists in Luray, and in countless areas of our country, the absence of African American churches, stores, and homes from East Main Street in tourism texts, and the dominance of Confederate memory—especially through the two prominent soldier monuments—reinforces that white history only is worth commemorating and celebrating. Their project, according to their comments in the booklet, helped them to realize that history can be made in other parts of the landscape—in this case, restaurants and the theatre—and that these everyday landscapes are, nonetheless, important to the myriad ways their informants experience history and memory.

The history displayed on the commemorative landscapes of Luray is ideological and exclusive. It tells of the personal sacrifices of early German-Swiss ancestors and the heroism of Confederate soldiers, making it appear that these individuals were solely responsible for Luray's history and present. That commemorative landscapes often show only limited perspectives of history and historical actors through various types of public history sites may seem overly critical. Public history sites, however, are anything but innocuous landmarks. Most of us are exposed to myriad historical sites daily, and they are tangible symbols that tourists and local citizens alike, even seventh graders, consider history markers. Through multiple discourses, including tourist brochures and books, historical narratives, historic designation efforts (including the Virginia Civil War Trails Program), public history sites are vital to how we learn and interpret history. But of the thousands of public history sites in this country, many continue to exhibit one-dimensional, white history, and these sites go unnoticed by visitors and local citizens.

A close look at many of the public history sites in Luray, including and especially ethnographic work, shows that African Americans were and are a part of Luray's history, and they deserve recognition in Luray's commemorative landscapes. Presently, the authenticity of the only public piece of African American history, the slave auction block, continues to be debated. Whether or not the block is authenticated, it stands as a subversive artifact—its presence questions the dominant forms of public history in Luray and demonstrates that quests for heritage are key to personal and community identity, a concept sometimes criticized by academics.

As I realized that Luray's commemorative landscapes smacked of racial exclusion, I also realized the possibility that African American history and heritage could be found in places other than public spaces. African American churches, as I assert, have a long tradition of heritage celebrations, including homecomings, events meaningful to southern African American culture, especially in Luray. Further, I noticed that local, state, and even federal organizations devoted to public history continue to designate the same kinds of events, people, and places as historic through "traditional" means: tangible monuments, houses, and exhibitions. Perhaps, however, it is time to look beyond this narrow type of commemoration and delve into other forms of expressing heritage. My study suggests that one of these forms could include the gospel performance by members of an African American choir held at the Mauck Meeting House during PCHA's annual Christmas pageants, and the homecoming celebrations of the New York-Virginia Club. Expanding the definitions of heritage and history is crucial today since marginalized racial and ethnic groups are demanding a presence on this country's public history landscapes.

Tourism, a topic critical to a study of public history in Luray since the town has served as a tourist destination for over one hundred years, can also benefit from becoming more inclusive both in practice and academically. Tourism is a key component to economic development in Page County, and over the past century, Luray has depended on the tourist dollar. In fact, as I argue, Luray's citizens have resisted cultural commodification, and, instead, have asserted community notions of heritage as opposed to creating traditions for tourists and the other outsiders who have visited this area of the Shenandoah Valley. Luray's tourism history provides an excellent example of a community where the term "tourism impact," as theorized by Quetzil Castenada, can be questioned. As I discussed, Luray's citizens, even at the onset of mass tourism in the late nineteenth century, held strong, even resistant notions of local and southern heritage, especially through the dedication of the Barbee monument in 1898. As scores of visitors traveled through the small town, altering the economy and way of life, historical evidence reveals that many of Luray's citizens used tourism to improve the town's infrastructure and to better individual lives through working in the trade. Thus, tourism yields not simply one-sided "impacts" but multidimensional and dynamic relationships.

Many tourism studies based on marginalized communities focus attention on the perceived and actual exploitative effects of tourism. Although this paradigm has been questioned over the past twenty years or so, tourism scholarship has not fully incorporated historical or diachronic perspectives, and has not theorized race and tourism, particularly tourism during segregation. Perhaps one of the best methods for reconfiguring approaches to tourism scholarship is to study local communities *over time.* Many articles and books that deal with specific geographical regions and tourism exist, but few look at the history of tourism in these particular areas. Examining how and why tourism has changed (i.e. tourist demographics, the construction and/or destruction of visitor centers) promotes a more dynamic and nuanced view of the effects of tourism. This type of view, in turn, can help to lay a framework with which to construct contemporary solutions to tourism challenges in a given community.

The absence of the African American experience in the scholarship of tourism is due, in part, to an academic assumption that a large, generalized socioeconomic group—the white middle class—is the main type of tourist. And while scholarship in the past twenty to thirty years has successfully incorporated postmodern theory to more fully investigate epistemologies of tourism, it has also neglected racial and ethnic diversity. When I discovered that African Americans traveled to and around Luray and the SNP, I did not consider, at first, that their roles as tourists would be different from whites. But as I talked to white and African American informants who told me about hidden spaces like Miss Martha's "Black Holiday Inn" and the back doors African Americans entered to buy food in the restaurants on Main Street in town, I realized that racism defined the experience of the African American traveler and tourist during segregation. Tourism scholarship that includes studies of tourism during segregation and/or a focus on racial and ethnic diversity in the past and the present will lead to a more complete understanding of tourism and tourism history, but may also encourage racial, ethnic, and cultural understanding. Again, perhaps a more localized and diachronic study of tourism combined with ethnographic work would provide the basis for developing a more inclusive tourism studies model.

Tourism scholarship has also not dealt with a novel type of tourist—the postmodern tourist. Many of my informants did not have complaints about the daily tourists, as I assumed they would going into my fieldwork. Instead, they discussed the "come heres" in derogatory ways, believing their biggest flaw was their desire to change "things" in Luray, perhaps even the town's agricultural character. Tourism studies need to embrace this kind of tourist since the threat of sprawl in rural areas is potentially a serious side effect of urban dwellers seeking out rural communities in which to live.

In considering commemorative landscapes, race, and tourism, I utilized postmodern theory, especially the idea of how public history and touristic sites can be political and ideological, and created by dominant, most often white groups in a community. These groups, relying on a hegemony of genealogy (as in Luray), can trace their ancestors back to the settlement of the town to justify that they are the rightful inheritors of the land and of history. Michel Foucault deconstructs genealogy by arguing that history is not linear and pre-determined, but accidental and incidental, hidden in social and cultural peripheries. Certainly an investigation of African Americans in Luray reveals that their history exists in these marginalized spaces.

A successful African American heritage preservation program that focuses on recapturing heritage should begin in local communities (like Luray) and with ethnographic work. Since many African American expressions of heritage and culture have had to remain private and in an oral realm for survival, one of the only methods of retrieving them is through performing ethnography. I recovered most of my information on the history of African Americans in Luray through informants who drove me to remote places on the landscape, who invited me into their homes and churches, and corresponded with me over the Internet. Concerted and localized efforts centered on ethnography can help to unearth African American history and heritage, while simultaneously showing to informants that their history does matter—that even a scrapbook of photos or newspaper clippings have the potential for creating the foundations of African American preservation efforts. Exploring private spaces and landscapes, however, has its caveats. As I discovered, driving or walking through unfamiliar territory can be dangerous, especially when one is an outsider to a culture, but most importantly, ethnographers must respect the very private and, often, sacred spaces they have found. Since the church is a crucial heritage space for many African Americans, preservation of these older structures, especially in Luray should be sought. But discussions with the church communities also need to be performed so that they can determine how preservation can take place around their worship practices.

By combining ethnography with cultural landscape study and traditional historical methods and theory, I gained a more comprehensive understanding of the politics of public history and its effects on the local community. Through ethnography I not only unearthed new information on public history and history, especially African American history, but I gained a perspective on how these sites are viewed and interpreted within Luray. The controversy over the Barbee monument rededication in 1998, for example, and the dedication of the slave auction block on the same day, as well as the racialized component of public history in Luray would not have become evident if I had simply relied on written documentation only. As well, the increasing problem (as the locals see it) with postmodern tourists would never have been realized if I had not pursued ethnographic work.

Working directly in the community also allowed me to observe current interpretive efforts where the potential exists to practice more inclusive heritage in some of its public history sites. Behind the library lies Luray's historic train depot, briefly described in chapter one. Taking a cue from other rural towns in Virginia that have successfully renovated train stations to promote tourism, the PCHA, the Railroad Heritage Group of Luray, and the town itself are working diligently to raise the money to finance the restoration of this important public history site. The plans call for the depot to serve as a visitor's center, archival reading room, and interpretive space, with the hope that this effort will light a spark in the tourism market. Approximately one hundred feet from the depot lies the slave auction block, a public history site that is sure to attract visitors, especially now that bright wreaths adorn it. Thus, the depot will have to share commemorative space with the block and share tourists.

The train depot could exhibit and interpret to both local citizens and to tourists the shared history and heritage present in this structure: in the 1940s, the time period the PCHA wishes to reconstruct the building to represent, the depot contained a "colored" waiting room. By interpreting this space as it was—a segregated structure—perhaps the depot could exhibit not only a more accurate picture of history, but could demonstrate how far the community and the nation have come, and how much farther they could go in terms of race relations. By including oral histories of African Americans who remember sitting

Epilogue

in the "colored" section, for example, the depot could offer a more inclusive and complex view of history.[1] In chapter six I demonstrated how the new exhibition in the SNP, which looks critically at history and historical actors, has received insightful and favorable reviews, revealing that people are willing to face controversial history. The exhibition does not, however, include a discussion of African Americans in the Valley, including their role as tourists in the SNP, a subject that should and could be explored.

The Civil War Trails Markers program could also benefit from including African American interpretation. Instead of simply noting the historical event(s) that took place on a given spot, perhaps the markers could include information on the diversity of the population, including stories of individual residents, white and African American, who lived in a given spot and their roles in and relationships to the Civil War.

Finally, in pursuing African American history we must realize that the quest is not simply about exposing a marginalized culture, but also about exposing more of white history too. The more we understand how shared our history and heritage actually are, the better equipped we will be to work together to integrate our country's commemorative landscapes well into the twenty-first century.

NOTE

1. Perhaps the new "West Luray Remembered" project could assist in this effort.

Bibliography

Manuscript Sources

Page County Public Library. Research Files. Luray, VA.
Page County Public Library. Microfilm Collection of *Page News & Courier.* Luray, VA.
Shenandoah National Park. Oral History Collection. Shenandoah National Park Archives, Luray, VA.
Shenandoah National Park. Research Files. Shenandoah National Park Archives, Luray, VA.

Primary Sources

Aunt Betty's Story: The Narrative of Bethany Veney, A Slave Woman. Luray: Page County Heritage Association, 1999.
Baumgartner, Mary. Interview by the author. 4 February 1999.
Baxter, Beatrice. Interview by the author. 13 May 2000.
Boswell, Jocelyn. Letter to the author. September 2000.
Butler, Carl. Interview by the author. 26 July 1999.
Concerned Citizens for Equality. "Meeting Notes for 8 July 1999." Luray: Concerned Citizens for Equality, 1999.
"Confederate Monument, Luray, Virginia, Herbert Barbee Sculptor," booklet of reprinted material from 21 July 1898 dedication. Luray: Page County Heritage Association, 1998.
Cooper, Christine. Interview by the author. 28 December 2000.
Corbin, Virgil. Interview with Dorothy Noble Smith. Luray: Shenandoah National Park Archives, 1979.
Curtis, Gale. Interview by the author. 22 June 1999.
Fant, Susan Braselton and Preservation Partners, LLC. "Interpretation Summary Sheet, Shenandoah Valley Battlefields National Historic District Commission." Richmond: Preservation Partners, LLC, December 1999.

———. "Shenandoah Valley Battlefields National Historic District Commission Summary Report of 30-Day Public Comment Period for Phase Two of the Action Plan: Developing Options and Strategies." Richmond: Preservation Partners, LLC, November 1999.

Goodwin, Richard. Interview by the author. 3 August 1999.

Gurnee, Russell H. *Discovery of Luray Caverns, Virginia.* Closter: R.H. Gurnee, 1978.

Gustavson, Jerry. Interview by the author. July 1999.

Hanson, Charlotte. Interview by the author. October 2000.

Hart, Frank. E-mails to the author. 1999–2001.

Interesting Page County Landmarks. Luray: Page County Heritage Association, n.d.

"Isabella Furnace and Settlement." Information Sheet given to author by Terry Nale, Historian, n.d.

Jones, Wanda. Interview by the author. 24 July 2001.

Kittell, Howard J. Letter to the author. 17 May 1999.

"Luray Caverns Backgrounder." Luray: Luray Caverns Corporation, n.d.

Maloney, Richard. E-mail to the author. 2 January 2000; February 2000; March 2000.

Michaels, Karla. Interview by the author. 28 December 2000.

Monroe, Bill. Interview by the author. June 1999.

The Negro Motorist Green Book. New York: Victor H. Green, 1948.

"Notice of Agricultural Operations." Luray: Board of Supervisors, County of Page, Virginia, 9 July 1999.

Page: The County of Plenty. Page County: Page County Bicentennial Commission, 1976.

Pezzoni, Dan and Leslie Giles. *Page County Architectural Survey Report.* Winchester: Landmark Associates, 1999.

Pollock, George Freeman. *Skyland: The Heart of the Shenandoah National Park.* Chesapeake Book Company, 1960.

Sandler, Richard. Interview by the author. 22 June 1999.

The Sentinel: The Page County Civil War Commission Newsletter 1 (1999): 1.

Skyland, situated on high plateau in the Blue Ridge near grand old Stony Man Peak. Roanoke: The Stone Printing and Manufacturing Co., 1919.

Starrs, Dr. James et al. "The Slave Auction Block of Luray, Virginia: A Report on the September 18, 1999 Investigation." Washington, DC: The George Washington University, Department of Forensic Anthropology, 2000.

Strickler, Harry. *A Short History of Page County, Virginia.* Richmond: Dietz Press, 1952.

———. *Massanutten, Settled by the Pennsylvania Pilgrim, 1726: The First White Settlement in the Shenandoah Valley.* Knightstown, IN: The Bookmark, 1978.

"Survey of Rural Mountain Settlement," Colonial Williamsburg, http://www.history .org/cwf/argy/argyshen.htm (22 April 2000).

Sutcliffe, Andrea. *Touring the Shenandoah Valley Backroads.* Winston-Salem: John F. Blair, 1999.

Thomas, Charlie. Interview by the author. June 1999.

"Through the Shenandoah Valley, Through the Uplands of Virginia." New York: Shenandoah Valley Railroad Co., circa 1910.

Wayland, John W. *Twenty-Five Chapters on the Shenandoah Valley.* Strasburg, VA: Shenandoah Publishing House, Inc., 1957.
———. *The German Elements of the Shenandoah Valley.* Published by author, 1907.
West Luray Remembered. Luray: Luray Elementary, 2001.
"What Ever Happened to the Luray Museum?" in *Page County Heritage Association Newsletter.* Luray: Page County Heritage Association, June 2000.

Secondary Sources

Althusser, Louis. "Ideology and Ideological State Apparatuses." In *Lenin and Philosophy.* Translated by Ben Brewster. New York: Monthly Review Press, 1971.
Ames, Michael. *Cannibal Tours and Glass Boxes: The Anthropology of Museums.* Vancouver: University of British of Columbia Press, 1992.
———. *Museums, the Public, and Anthropology: A Study in the Anthropology of Anthropology.* Vancouver, University of British of Columbia Press, 1986.
Anderson, Benedict. *Imagined Communities.* New York: Verso, 1983.
Appadurai, Arjun. *The Social Life of Things.* New York: Cambridge, 1986.
Atwood, Elizabeth Ann. "'Saratoga of the South'" Tourism in Luray, Virginia, 1878–1905." Master's Thesis, University of Virginia, Corcoran Department of History, May 1983.
Ballard, Charles C. "Dismissing the Peculiar Institution: Assessing Slavery in Page and Rockingham Counties, Virginia." Luray, VA: Page County Heritage Association, 1999.
———. "From Iron Plantation to Company Town: The Shenandoah Iron Works, 1836–1907." Luray, VA: Page County Heritage Association, 1999.
Barker, Gary. *The Handcraft Revival in Southern Appalachia, 1930–1960.* Knoxville: University of Tennessee Press, 1991.
Barnett, Steve and Martin Silverman. "Separations in Capitalist Societies: Persons, Things, Units, and Relations." In *Ideology and Everyday Life.* Edited by Steve Barnett and Martin Silverman. Ann Arbor: University of Michigan Press, 1979.
Barrell, John. *The Dark Side of the Landscape: The Rural Poor in English Painting 1730–1840.* New York: Cambridge University Press, 1980.
Batteau, Allen W. *The Invention of Appalachia.* Tucson: University of Arizona Press, 1990.
Baudrillard, Jean. *Selected Writings.* Stanford: Stanford University Press, 1988.
———. *For a Critique of the Political Economy of the Sign.* St. Louis: Telos Press, 1981.
Bauman, Richard, Roger Abrahams, with Susan Kalcik. "American Folklore and American Studies." *American Quarterly* (Bibliography Issue 1976): 360–77.
Becker, Jane Stewart. "Selling Traditions: The Domestication of Southern Appalachian Culture in 1930s America." (Ph.D. diss.) Boston University, 1993.
——— and Barbara Franco. *Folk Roots, New Roots: Folklore in American Life.* Lexington, MA: Museum of Our National Heritage, 1988.
Ben-Amos, Dan. "The Seven Strands of Tradition: Varities in its Meaning in American Folklore Studies." *Journal of Folklore Research* 21 (May–December, 1984): 97–131.

Bendix, Regina. "Folklorism: The Challenge of a Concept." *International Folklore Review* 6 (1988): 5–15.

———. "Tourism and Cultural Displays: Inventing Traditions for Whom?" *Journal of American Folklore* 102 (April/June 1989): 131–46.

Bendix. Reinhard. "Tradition and Modernity Reconsidered." *Comparative Studies in Society and History* 9 (April 1967): 292–346.

Benson, Susan Porter et al. *Presenting the Past: Essays on History and the Public.* Philadelphia: Temple University Press, 1986.

Berkhofer, Robert F. "The Challenge of Poetics to (Normal) Historical Practice." *Poetics Today* 9:2 (1988): 435–52.

Bertaux, Daniel, ed. *Biography and Society: The Life History Approach.* Beverly Hills: Sage Publications, 1981.

Bodnar, John. *Remaking America: Public Memory, Commemoration, and Patriotism in the Twentieth Century.* Princeton: Princeton University Press, 1992.

Boorstin, Daniel. *The Image: A Guide to Pseudo-Events in America.* New York: Harper, 1964.

Brandt, John. "Unemployment: The Theme Park." *New York Times Magazine,* August 4, 1996: 46–47.

Brewer, John and Roy Porter, eds. *Consumption and World of Goods.* New York: Routledge, 1993.

Bronner, Simon J. *Grasping Things: Folk Material Culture and Mass Society in America.* Lexington, KY: University Press of Kentucky, 1986.

Brown, Dona. *Inventing New England: Regional Tourism in the Nineteenth Century.* Washington, DC: Smithsonian Institution Press, 1995.

Brundage, W. Fitzhugh, ed. *Where These Memories Grow: History, Memory, and Southern Identity.* Chapel Hill: University of North Carolina Press, 2000.

Campbell, Colin. *The Romantic Ethic and the Spirit of Modern Consumerism.* New York: Basil Blackwell, 1987.

Campbell, Edward D.C. Jr. with Kym S. Rice. *Before Freedom Came: African American Life in the Antebellum South.* Richmond: Museum of the Confederacy, 1991.

Carson, Barbara. "Interpreting History Through Objects." *Journal of Museum Education* 10:3 (1985): 129–33.

Carson, Cary. "The Consumer Revolution in Colonial British America: Why Demand?" In *Of Consuming Interests: The Style of Life in the Eighteenth Century.* Edited by Cary Carson, Ronald Hoffman, and Peter Albert. Charlottesville: University Press of Virginia, 1994.

———. "Lost in the Fun House: A Commentary on Anthropologists' First Contact With History Museums." *The Journal of American History.* 81 (1994): 137–50.

Castaneda, Quetzil E. *In the Museum of Maya Culture: Touring Chichen Itza.* Minneapolis: Regents of the University of Minnesota, 1996.

Chambers, Erve, ed. *Tourism and Culture: An Applied Perspective.* Albany: State University of New York Press, 1997.

Clark-Lewis, Elizabeth. *Living In, Living Out: African-American Domestics and the Great Migration.* New York: Kodansha American, Inc. 1994.

Cohen, Erik. "A Phenomenology of Tourist Types." *Sociology.* 13 (1979): 170–201.

———. "Authenticity and Commoditization in Tourism." *Annals of Tourism Research.* 15 (1998): 371–86.

———. "Traditions in the Qualitative Sociology of Tourism." *Annals of Tourism Research.* 15 (1988): 29–46.

Cole, Douglas. *Captured Heritage: The Scramble for Northwest Coast Artifacts.* Seattle: University of Washington Press, 1985.

Crandall, Hugh and Reed Engle. *Shenandoah: The Story Behind the Scenery.* Las Vegas: KC Publications, Inc., 1990.

Crew, Spencer. "People, Places, Perspectives: Another Look at the Founding Fathers." *Palimpsest* 72:4 (1991): 163–75.

Cronon, William. "The Trouble With Nature." In *The Best American Essays 1996.* Edited by Geoffrey C. Ward. New York: Houghton Mifflin, 1996.

Csikszentmihalyi, Mihalyi and Eugene Rochberg-Halton. *The Meaning of Things: Domestic Symbols and the Self.* 1981.

Deetz, James. *In Small Things Forgotten: The Archaeology of Early American Life.* Garden City, NY: Anchor Press/Doubleday, 1977.

Dew, Charles B. *Bond of Iron: Master and Slave at Buffalo Forge.* New York: W. W. Norton, 1994.

Dilworth, Leah. *Imagining Indians in the Southwest: Persistent Visions of a Primitive Past.* Washington, DC: Smithsonian Institution Press, 1996.

Dominiquez, Virginia. "The Marketing of Heritage." *American Ethnologist* 13 (August 1986): 546–55.

Dorson, Richard. "Folkore and Fakelore." *American Mercury* 70 (1950): 335–43.

Dorst, John D. *The Written Suburb: An American Site, An Ethnographic Dilemma.* Philadelphia: University of Pennsylvania Press, 1989.

Douglas, Mary and Baron Isherwood. *The World of Goods: Towards an Anthropology of Consumption.* London: Allen Lane, 1979.

Eaton, Allen. *Handicrafts of the Southern Highlands.* New York: Dover, 1973.

Engle, Reed L. "Shenandoah: Laboratory for Change." *CRM: Cultural Resources Management: Shenandoah: Managing Cultural Resources in a Natural Park* 21 (1998): 34–35.

Evans-Pritchard, Dierdre. "The Portal Case: Authenticity, Tourism, Traditions, and the Law." *Journal of American Folklore* 100 (1987): 287–96.

Fabian, Johannes. *Time and the Other: How Anthropology Makes Its Object.* New York: Columbia University Press, 1983.

Fabre, Genevieve and Robert O'Meally, eds. *History & Memory in African American Culture.* New York: Oxford University Press, 1994.

Foucault, Michel. *Language, Counter-Memory, Practice: Selected Essays and Interviews.* Edited by Donald F. Bouchard. Ithaca: Cornell University Press, 1977.

———. *The Order of Things: An Archaeology of the Human Sciences.* New York: Random House, 1973.

Fox, Richard Wightman and T.J. Jackson Lears, eds. *The Culture of Consumption: Critical Essays in American History 1880–1980.* New York: Pantheon, 1983.

Friedman, Jonathan. "The Past in the Future: History and the Politics of Identity." *American Anthropologist* 94 (4) (1992): 837–59.

Gable, Eric and Richard Handler. "The Authority of Documents at Some American History Museums." *The Journal of American History* 81 (1994): 119–36.

Gillis, John, ed. *Commemorations: The Politics of National Identity.* Princeton: Princeton University Press, 1994.

Glassie, Henry. "Meaningful Things and Appropriate Myths: The Artifact's Place in American Studies." *Prospects* 3 (1977): 1–49.

——. *Folk Housing in Middle Virginia.* Knoxville: University of Tennessee Press, 1975.

Goffman, Erving. *The Presentation of Self in Everyday Life.* New York: Doubleday, 1959.

Gundaker, Grey, ed. *Keep Your Head to the Sky: Interpreting African American Home Ground.* Charlottesville: University Press of Virginia, 1998.

Habermas, Jurgen. *Legitimation Crisis.* T. McCarthy, trans. Boston: Beacon Press, 1973.

Handler, Richard. *Nationalism and the Politics of Culture in Quebec.* Madison, WI: University of Wisconsin Press, 1988.

Handler, Richard and Eric Gable. *The New History in an Old Museum: Creating the Past at Colonial Williamsburg.* Durham: Duke University Press, 1997.

Handler, Richard and William Saxton. "Dyssimulation: Reflexivity, Narrative, and the Quest for Authenticity in 'Living History.'" *Cultural Anthropology* 3 (1988): 242–65.

Harkin, Michael. "Modernist Anthropology and Tourism of the Authentic." *Annals of Tourism Research* 22 (1995): 650–70.

Herzfeld, Michael. *Ours Once More: Folklore, Ideology, and the Making of Modern Greece.* Austin: University of Texas Press, 1982.

Hobsbawn, Eric and Terence Ranger. *The Invention of Tradition.* Cambridge, England: Cambridge University Press, 1983.

Hodder, Ian. "Post-modernism, Post-structualism, and Post-processual Archaeology." In Ian Hodder, ed., *The Meaning of Things.* London: Unwin-Hymen, 1986.

Horwitz, Tony. *Confederates in the Attic: Dispatches From the Unfinished Civil War.* New York: Vintage Books, 1999.

Irwin, William. *The New Niagara: Tourism, Technology, and the Landscape of Niagara Falls: 1776–1917.* University Park, PA: Pennsylvania State University Press, 1996.

Isaac, Rhys. *The Transformation of Virginia: 1740–1790.* New York: W.W. Norton & Co., 1982.

——. "Ethnographic Method in History: An Action Approach." In Robert Blair St. George, ed., *Material Life in America: 1600–1860.* Boston: Northeastern University Press, 1988.

Jameson, Frederic. *Postmodernism, or, the Cultural Logic of Late Capitalism.* Durham: Duke University Press, 1995.

Jones, Alfred Haworth. "The Search for a Usable Past in the New Deal Era." *American Quarterly* 23 (December 1971): 710–24.

Kammen, Michael. *Mystic Chords of Memory.* New York: First Vintage, 1991.

Karp, Ivan and Steven D. Levine, eds. *Exhibiting Cultures: The Poetics and Politics of Museum Display.* Washington, DC: Smithsonian Institution Press, 1991.

Kirshenblatt-Gimblett, Barbara. *Destination Culture: Tourism, Museums, and Culture.* Berkeley: University of California Press, 1998.

Koons, Kenneth and Warren R. Hofstra, eds. *After the Backcountry: Rural Life in the Great Valley of Virginia, 1800–1900.* Knoxville: University of Tennessee Press, 2000.

Korr, Jeremy. "A Proposed Model for Landscape Study." *Material Culture* 29 (1997): 1–18.

Lambert, Darwin. *The Undying Past of Shenandoah National Park.* Boulder: Roberts Rinehart, Inc. 1989.

Lassiter, Barbara Babcock. *American Wilderness: The Hudson River School of Painting.* Garden City, NY: 1978.

Lawson, Karol Ann Peard. "An Inexhaustible Abundance: The National Landscape Depicted in American Magazines: 1780–1820." *Journal of the Early Republic* 21 (Fall 1992): 303–30.

Lears, T.J. Jackson. *No Place of Grace: Antimodernism and the Transformation of American Culture.* New York: Pantheon, 1981.

Leone, Mark P. "The Relationship Between Artifacts and the Public in Outdoor History Museums." *Annals of the New York Academy of Sciences* 376 (1981): 301–14.

———. "An Archaeology of DeWitt Wallace Gallery at Colonial Williamsburg." In *Museums and the Appropriation of Culture.* Edited by Susan Pearce. London: Athone, 1994.

———. Exhibition Review. *Journal of American History* (1992): 1082–87.

Leone, Mark P. and Neil Asher Silberman, eds. *Invisible America: Unearthing Our Hidden History.* New York: Henry Holt, 1995.

Levine, Lawrence W. *Black Culture and Black Consciousness: Afro-American Folk Thought From Slavery to Freedom.* New York: Oxford University Press, 1977.

Levinson, Sanford. *Written in Stone: Public Monuments in Changing Societies.* Durham: Duke University Press, 1998.

Loewen, James W. *Lies Across America: What Our Historic Sites Get Wrong.* New York: The New Press, 1999.

Loth, Calder. *Virginia Landmarks of Black History.* Charlottesville: University of Virginia Press, 1995.

Lowenthal, David. *The Past Is a Foreign Country.* New York: Cambridge University Press, 1985.

———. *Possessed by the Past: The Heritage Crusade and the Spoils of History.* New York: Free Press, 1996.

———. "Past Time, Present Place: Landscape and Memory," *The Geographical Review* LXV (January 1975), 1–36.

———. "The American Way of History." *Columbia University Forum*, Summer (1966): 27–32.

Lubar, Steven and W. David Kingery, eds. *History From Things: Essays on Material Culture.* Washington, DC: Smithsonian Institution Press, 1993.

MacCannell, Dean. *Empty Meeting Grounds: The Tourist Papers.* New York: Routledge, 1992.

———. *The Tourist: A New Theory of the Leisure Class.* New York: Schoken Books, 1989.

———. "Reconstructed Ethnicity: Tourism and Cultural Identity in Third World Communities." *Annals of Tourism Research* 11 (1984): 375–91.

Marcus, George and M.J. Fischer. *Anthropology as Cultural Critique: An Experimental Moment in the Human Sciences.* Chicago: University of Chicago Press, 1986.

Martin, Ann Smart. "Makers, Buyers, and Users: Consumerism as a Material Culture Framework." *Winterthur Portfolio* 28 (1993): 141–57.

Martin, Ann Smart and J. Ritchie Garrison, eds. *American Material Culture: The Shape of the Field.* Delaware: Henry Francis DuPont Winterthur Museum, 1997.

McCay, Ian. *The Quest of the Folk: Antimodernism and Cultural Selection in Twentieth-Century Nova Scotia.* Montreal: McGill-Queens University Press, 1994.

McNeil, W.K. *Appalachian Images in Folk and Popular Culture.* Knoxville: University of Tennessee Press, 1995.

Meinig, D.W. "The Beholding Eye: Ten Versions of the Same Scene." In D.W. Meinig, editor. *The Interpretation of Ordinary Landscapes: Geographical Essays.* New York: Oxford University Press, 1979.

Miller, Daniel. *Material Culture and Mass Consumption.* Oxford: Basil Blackwell, 1987.

Noblitt, Phil. "The Blue Ridge Parkway and Myths of the Pioneer." *Appalachian Journal.* Summer (1994): 394–409.

Norkunas, Martha. *The Politics of Public Memory: Tourism, History, and Ethnicity* in *Monterey, California.* Albany: SUNY Press, 1993.

Novak, Barbara. *Nature and Culture: American Landscape and Painting, 1825–1875.* New York: Oxford University Press, 1980.

Olson, Ted. *Blue Ridge Folklife.* Jackson: University Press of Mississippi, 1998.

Pearce, Susan M. *Museum Studies in Material Culture.* Washington, DC: Smithsonian Institution Press, 1991.

Piehler, G. Kurt. *Remembering War the American Way.* Washington, DC: Smithsonian Institution Press, 1995.

Powell, Douglas Reichert. "Mapping Appalachia." *Southern Exposure* 24 (1996): 47–51.

Reeder, Carolyn and Jack. *Shenandoah Secrets: The Story of the Park's Hidden Past.* Washington, DC: Potomac Appalachian Trail Club, 1991.

———. *Shenandoah Vestiges: What the Mountain People Left Behind.* Washington, DC: Potomac Appalachian Trail Club, 1980.

———. *Shenandoah Heritage: The Story of the People Before the Park.* Washington, DC: Potomac Appalachian Trail Club, 1978.

Rosenzweig, Roy, and David Thelen. *The Presence of the Past: Popular Uses of History in American Life.* New York: Columbia University Press, 1998.

Savage, Kirk. *Standing Soldiers, Kneeling Slaves: Race, War, and Monument in Nineteenth-Century America.* Princeton: Princeton University Press, 1995.

Schlereth, Thomas J. *Material Culture: A Research Guide.* Lawrence, KS: University Press of Kansas, 1985.

———. *Victorian America: Transformations in Everyday Life, 1876–1915*. New York: Harper Perennial, 1991.

———. *Artifacts and the American Past*. Nashville: American Association of State and Local History, 1980.

Schlereth, Thomas J., ed. *Material Culture Studies in America*. Nashville: American Association of State and Local History, 1981.

Schlereth, Thomas J. and Barbara Allen, eds. *Sense of Place: American Regional Cultures*. Lexington, KY: University Press of Kentucky, 1990.

Shackel, Paul A. *Memory in Black and White: Race, Commemoration, and the Post-Bellum Landscape*. Walnut Creek, CA: AltaMira Press, 2003.

Shanks, Michael and Christopher Tilley. *Social Theory and Archaeology*. Albuquerque: University of New Mexico Press, 1993.

———. *Presenting the Past: Re-Constructing Archaeology*. New York: Routledge, 1992.

———. "Hermeneutics, Dialectics, and Archaeology," In *Reconstructing Archaeology*. New York: Routledge, 1992.

Sherman, Daniel J. and Irit Rogoff, eds. *Museum Culture: Histories, Discourses, Spectacles*. Minneapolis: University of Minnesota Press, 1994.

Shi, David. *The Simple Life: Plain Living and High Thinking in American Culture*. New York: Oxford University Press, 1985.

Shklar, Judith N. "Subversive Geneaologies." In *Myth, Symbol, and Culture*. Edited by Clifford Geertz. New York: W.W. Norton, 1971.

Sies, Mary Corbin. "Toward a Performance Theory of the Suburban Ideal, 1877–1917," in Thomas Carter and Bernard Herman, eds., *Perspectives in Vernacular Architecture IV*. St. Louis: University of Missouri Press, 1991.

Simmons, J. Suzanne. "They Too Were Here: African-Americans in Augusta County and Staunton, Virginia, 1745–1865." Master's Thesis, James Madison University, May 1994.

Smith, Valene, ed. *Hosts and Guests: The Anthropology of Tourism*. Philadelphia: University of Pennsylvania Press, 1989.

St. George, Robert, ed. *Material Life in America 1600–1800*. Boston: Northeastern University Press, 1988.

Thomas, Jim. *Doing Critical Ethnography*. Newbury Park: Sage Publications, 1993.

Thompson, Spurgeon. "The Romance of Simulation: W.B. Yeats and the Theme-Parking of Ireland." *Eire*, Spring (1995): 17–34.

Tilley, Christopher, ed. *Reading Material Culture*. Basil Blackwell: Cambridge, MA, 1990.

———. *The Phenomenology of Landscape: Places, Paths, Monuments*. Providence, RI: Berg, 1994.

———. "Interpreting Material Culture." In Ian Hodder, ed. *The Meaning of Things*. London: Unwin-Hymen, 1986.

Upton, Dell and John Michael Vlach. *Common Places: Readings in Vernacular Architecture*. Athens, GA: University of Georgia Press, 1986.

Urry, John. *Consuming Places*. New York: Routledge, 1995.

———. *The Tourist Gaze: Leisure Travel in Contemporary Societies*. London: Sage, 1990.

Urry, John and Chris Rojek, eds. *Touring Cultures: Transformations of Travel and Theory.* London: Routledge, 1997.

Veblen, Thorstein. *Theory of the Leisure Class.* New York: Penguin, 1967.

Vlach, John Michael. *The Afro-American Tradition in Decorative Arts.* Athens, GA: Brown Thrasher Books, 1978.

Wallace, Michael. "Mickey Mouse History: Portraying the Past at Disney World." *Radical History Review* 32 (1985): 33–57.

———. "Visiting the Past: History Museums in the United States." *Radical History Review* 25 (1981): 63–96.

Walsh, Kevin. *The Representation of the Past: Museums and Heritage in the Postmodern World.* New York: Routledge, 1992.

Watkins, Charles A. "Merchandising the Mountaineer: Photography, The Great Depression, and *Cabins in the Laurel. Appalachian Journal* 12 (1985): 215–38.

Whisnant, David. *All That Is Native and Fine.* The Politics of Culture of an American Region. Chapel Hill: University of North Carolina Press, 1983.

———. "Ethnicity and the Recovery of Regional Identity in Appalachia." In *The Rediscovery of Ethnicity,* edited by Sallie TeSelle. New York: Harper and Row, 1973.

Williams, Michael Ann. *Homeplace: The Social Use and Meaning of the Folk Dwelling in Southwestern North Carolina.* Athens, GA: University of Georgia Press, 1991.

Williams, Raymond. *The Country and the City.* New York: Oxford University Press, 1975.

Williamson, J.W. *Hillbillyland: What the Movies Did to the Mountains & What the Mountains Did to the Movies.* Chapel Hill: University of North Carolina Press, 1995.

Index